World War 2 Heroes

Uncover Extraordinary Stories of Courage, Sacrifice, and Valor

Table of Contents

Introduction

World War II was a paradigm-shifting occurrence that formed many of the international institutions governing global relations today. The genocide of millions of Jewish people is still one of the most horrific atrocities the world has ever encountered. The scenes from concentration camps are nightmare-inducing visions and instances of sorrow and suffering. The Nazi military was one of the most technologically advanced and disciplined forces the world has ever seen. Defeating them sometimes seemed impossible, but the Allies emerged victorious with resilience, determination, and grit.

When referring to WWII, it is easy to get caught up in dates, timelines, and ideologies. However, humanity should never overlook the individual stories of honorable people who were on the ground fighting for freedom. This book recounts their tales of glory, failures, and sacrifice to give a detailed picture of what happened in the war and how the genocidal Nazi regime was eventually defeated. Inaction in the face of injustice is support for wickedness, so principled people had no choice but to do whatever they could to bring the atrocities of Nazi Germany to an end, whether by picking up arms or finding other ways to provide support.

The successful end of World War II was sown together by several interlocking parts, including generals, foot soldiers, and heads of state. The intellectual and strategic prowess of the planners, coupled with the unbreakable spirits of the men who charged the frontlines, ultimately determined how the world would be structured to this day. The foundation of the new civilization built post-war was poured with the blood of soldiers who fearlessly fought for their ideals despite great uncertainty. Bombs could not shatter their dreams, and the rattling bangs from machine guns could not silence their cries against oppression.

The relevance of WWII on global governance cannot be overstated. The actions of a handful of brave men and women reshaped society in ways unimaginable before the end of the war. Their stories must be kept alive to facilitate gratitude among modern people and ensure that past mistakes are never repeated. War is an ugly business but a recurring part of human existence. The touching stories of WWII heroes serve as a reminder that some things, like justice and freedom, are worth fighting for.

World War II is often discussed as nation-states fighting, giving it a grand, unrelatable facade. However, when you break it down to the level of individuals coming together and putting their lives on the line for a greater cause than themselves, you get a true sense of the gravity of global conflict. By retracing the dangerous steps made by key figures in the war, you get a glimpse into the terrifying conditions that birthed the highest potential of humankind in hopeless situations. Only in contrast to the darkest evil can the brightest lights shine into the eternity of civilizational memory.

Chapter 1: Winston Churchill: Britain's Indomitable Leader

Winston Churchill, an accurate depiction of 20th-century statesmanship, joined politics to become an enduring symbol of resilience and unwavering leadership. He was born on November 30, 1874, in the Blenheim Palace. His father, Randolph Churchill, was an elected member of parliament. From his paternal side, Churchill was a member of the aristocracy as the descendant of John Churchill. His grandfather, the Duke of Marlborough, was appointed as the ruler of Ireland, highlighting the family's deep roots in British politics. His multifaceted career spanned the military, literature, and politics, leaving his mark on each.

Winston Churchill, an accurate depiction of 20th-century statesmanship, joined politics to become an enduring symbol of resilience and unwavering leadership.
https://commons.wikimedia.org/wiki/File:Winston-Churchill-by-John-Lavery-(1916).jpg

Churchill's early military exploits, including his service in the Boer War and World War I, were the basis for his future goals. However, his eloquence would etch his name into the history books. A prolific writer and orator, Churchill's speeches boosted the British spirit during a crisis.

In the political arena, Churchill's career was illustrious and impactful. With his political struggle, he climbed the party rankings and served as First Lord of the Admiralty before resigning after the disastrous Gallipoli Campaign during World War I. Another notable political event was the warning Churchill gave about Nazi Germany and their plans to invade Europe. His claims of the rising threat were initially met with skepticism, but soon, his foresight became true when Hitler's forces swept across Europe.

During World War II, his leadership gained new heights of recognition. As Prime Minister from 1940 to 1945, he guided Britain through the intense conflict years with a steadfast resolve, earning him the admiration of allies and the grudging respect of enemies. His speeches, like the iconic *"We shall fight on the beaches,"* became the rallying cries of a nation facing existential threats.

Churchill's political career was marked by its peaks and valleys, culminating in his second term as Prime Minister in the 1950s. He advocated creating and maintaining a special relationship with allies like the United States. He used his political influence and status to shape the post-war world order.

Besides his achievements in politics and war, Churchill was a Nobel laureate in literature. His writings, including a six-volume history of World War II, are among his most known contributions to literature. Sir Winston Churchill, knighted in 1953, embodies the resilience of the human spirit and the power of leadership to shape the course of history.

Appointment as Prime Minister

Winston Churchill's appointment as Prime Minister in 1940 marked a critical turning point in World War II, as Britain faced dire wartime circumstances. His leadership during this period profoundly impacted the course of the war and established him as one of the most iconic figures in history. He took office on May 10, 1940, when the threat of Nazi invasion loomed large, and much of Europe had already fallen to German forces. The situation was dire, and the British Expeditionary Force was trapped at Dunkirk. In his first speech to the House of

Commons, Churchill famously declared, *"I have nothing to offer but blood, toil, tears, and sweat,"* setting the tone for impactful decisions and unwavering determination that would characterize his leadership.

Although countrymen able to fight were volunteering to join the army, Churchill, during that period, inspired and rallied the British people. His speeches, filled with passion and eloquence, skyrocketed morale and sparked a determination to fight for oneself, the people, and the homeland. The *"We shall fight on the beaches"* speech, delivered on June 4, 1940, remains one of his most iconic addresses, symbolizing the spirit of resistance against the Nazi onslaught. His strategic vision and diplomatic skills were evident in his alliances with key Allied leaders, particularly with U.S. President Franklin D. Roosevelt and Soviet Premier Joseph Stalin. His collaboration with Roosevelt resulted in the Atlantic Charter, a declaration of the Allies' post-war goals and commitment to defeating the Axis powers.

As Prime Minister, Churchill's role in the military decisions shaped the war's outcome. He was deeply involved in strategic planning and a driving force behind key operations, like the Battle of Britain, which thwarted the German Luftwaffe's attempts to gain air superiority over Britain. Churchill's insistence on the importance of the Mediterranean theater led to the successful North African campaign and the eventual defeat of Axis forces there. His strategic insight influenced the decision to launch the invasions of Sicily and Italy, paving the way for the Allied advance in Europe.

Perhaps Churchill's most enduring legacy is his unwavering commitment to victory, expressed in his famous words, *"We shall never surrender."* His leadership and determination during the darkest days of the war inspired the British people and Allied forces as they faced formidable challenges. After the war, his impact extended to the post-war order. He was vital in forming the United Nations, advocating for international cooperation to prevent future conflicts and promote peace.

Winston Churchill's pivotal role during World War II, from his appointment as Prime Minister in 1940 to the ultimate Allied victory, showcased his exceptional leadership, strategic acumen, and unyielding resolve. His legacy as one of the greatest wartime leaders endures, symbolizing the triumph of courage and determination in the face of adversity.

Rallying Efforts

Winston Churchill's immediate efforts to rally the nation during the early years of World War II were characterized by a resolute determination and an unparalleled ability to inspire. As he assumed the role of Prime Minister in 1940, facing the looming threat of Nazi invasion, Churchill wasted no time in delivering speeches that would become iconic symbols of British resistance. One of the most memorable addresses came on June 4, 1940, in the aftermath of the evacuation of British and Allied forces from Dunkirk. In his speech to the House of Commons, Churchill delivered the stirring words, *"We shall fight on the beaches, we shall fight on the landing grounds, we shall fight in the fields and in the streets, we shall fight in the hills; we shall never surrender."* This declaration of unwavering resolve became a rallying cry that encapsulated the spirit of defiance characterizing Britain's stance against Nazi aggression.

Another pivotal speech, delivered on June 18, 1940, is known as *"Their Finest Hour."* In this address, Churchill acknowledged the situation's gravity but bolstered the nation's morale by emphasizing the strength that could be drawn from adversity. He declared, *"Let us therefore brace ourselves to our duties, and so bear ourselves that if the British Empire and its Commonwealth last for a thousand years, men will still say, 'This was their finest hour."* These words served as a poignant reminder that even in the face of unprecedented challenges, the British people could rise to the occasion.

"We Shall Fight on the Beaches" and *"Their Finest Hour"* highlight Churchill's gift for stirring oratory and instilling hope in the face of adversity. These speeches resonated with the British public and transcended national borders, becoming symbolic expressions of the broader Allied resistance against the Axis powers. His immediate efforts to rally the nation through these iconic speeches solidified his reputation as a leader who could articulate the collective spirit of a nation at a crucial juncture in history.

The Grand Alliance

Winston Churchill's instrumental role in forming the "Grand Alliance" with the United States and the Soviet Union was a masterstroke that significantly contributed to the Allied victory in World War II. Recognizing the importance of a united front against the Axis powers, he worked tirelessly to build and maintain strategic alliances that would reshape the war's course.

Churchill's relationship with U.S. President Franklin D. Roosevelt was central to the Grand Alliance. Their rapport, forged through a series of correspondence known as the "Atlantic Charter," laid the foundation for a close collaboration between the United Kingdom and the United States. This alliance was crucial in providing the necessary resources, including military aid and economic support, to sustain the war effort. Simultaneously, Churchill understood the strategic imperative of aligning with the Soviet Union despite ideological differences. His meetings with Joseph Stalin, notably the Tehran Conference in 1943, helped solidify the Allies' commitment to a coordinated military strategy. The unity forged between the Western Allies and the Soviet Union became a linchpin in the ultimate defeat of Nazi Germany.

Churchill's military strategy was fundamental in making decisions during crucial battles and campaigns. The North African Campaign, where British forces, under the command of General Bernard Montgomery, decisively defeated German and Italian forces, showcased Churchill's strategic acumen. His insistence on prioritizing the Mediterranean theater and supporting Operation Torch, the Allied invasion of North Africa, demonstrated a farsighted understanding of the conflict's global nature.

The D-Day landings on June 6, 1944, marked another watershed moment in the war, and Churchill's influence was evident in the planning and execution of this ambitious operation. Code-named Operation Overlord, the Normandy landings were a joint effort involving British, American, and Canadian forces. Churchill's support for the invasion was unwavering, and his commitment to ensuring its success was substantial in the liberation of Western Europe from Nazi occupation.

Throughout these campaigns, Churchill's strategic decisions reflected a keen understanding of the geopolitical landscape and an unwavering commitment to the Allied cause. His leadership and influence in the Grand Alliance were essential in maintaining cohesion among the Allies and maximizing their collective military and economic strength. Winston Churchill's instrumental role in forming and sustaining the Grand Alliance with the United States and the Soviet Union and his strategic decisions during critical battles and campaigns solidified his legacy as a statesman whose vision and leadership significantly contributed to the

Allied victory in World War II.

Winston Churchill's participation in key wartime conferences, including those at Tehran and Yalta, marked pivotal moments where the foundations of post-war geopolitics were laid. Additionally, his efforts to maintain the cohesion of the British Empire during this tumultuous period highlighted his commitment to preserving the Commonwealth's global influence. The Tehran Conference of 1943 brought together the "Big Three" Allied leaders – Churchill, Franklin D. Roosevelt, and Joseph Stalin. Churchill's diplomatic skills were fully displayed as the leaders discussed coordinating military efforts and post-war planning. Despite their ideological differences, Churchill's ability to engage with Roosevelt and Stalin was crucial in fostering unity among the Allies. The Yalta Conference in 1945 further showcased his role in shaping the post-war order. While the Allied leaders discussed the division of Germany and the establishment of the United Nations, Churchill sought to ensure that Britain's interests and global influence were safeguarded. Although marked by tensions, the conference highlighted Churchill's determination to secure a future where democratic principles could prevail.

His commitment to maintaining the cohesion of the British Empire during World War II was evident in his efforts to rally the colonies and dominions. Recognizing the Commonwealth's importance, he sought to ensure the colonies' active participation in the war effort. The Empire Air Training Scheme and the contributions of Commonwealth forces in key theaters of war underscored Churchill's vision of a united front against the Axis powers.

Tehran Conference (1943)

The Tehran Conference in 1943 marked a critical juncture in World War II, bringing together the leaders of the Allied powers—Winston Churchill, Franklin D. Roosevelt, and Joseph Stalin. Churchill's participation in this conference was driven by a dual agenda: securing Stalin's commitment to opening a second front in Western Europe and fostering unity among the Allies. Churchill's diplomatic prowess was evident in the negotiations with Stalin. He navigated the delicate balance between the Western Allies' needs and the strategic considerations of the Eastern Front. The successful outcome included an agreement for the Normandy landings in 1944, an essential step toward defeating Nazi Germany. Beyond military strategy, Churchill strived to maintain unity among the Allies, emphasizing their shared goal despite ideological differences.

Maintaining the British Empire's Cohesion

Churchill recognized the importance of preserving the British Empire's cohesion throughout the war. His efforts were comprehensive. One significant initiative was the Empire Air Training Scheme, which aimed to strengthen ties within the Commonwealth. By training aircrews from various Commonwealth countries, Churchill fostered collaboration and reinforced the notion of a collective defense. Contributions from across the empire, including troops from India, Canada, Australia, and New Zealand, were crucial in different areas of the war. Additionally, Churchill convened Empire Conferences, providing a platform for Commonwealth leaders to discuss wartime strategy and post-war reconstruction. These gatherings were vital in maintaining unity within the empire.

Yalta Conference (1945)

The Yalta Conference of 1945, attended by Churchill, Roosevelt, and Stalin, focused on post-war issues as the conflict in Europe approached its conclusion. Churchill's role in this conference was marked by discussions on the division of Germany, the formation of the United Nations, and the fate of Eastern Europe. Addressing the division of Germany, Churchill collaborated with the other leaders to lay the groundwork for the country's occupation and administration post-war. Despite concessions made to Stalin in Eastern Europe, Churchill sought to uphold democratic ideals and ensure self-determination for nations in the region. The Yalta Conference also entered discussions on forming the United Nations, with Churchill advocating for an international organization to prevent future conflicts and promote global cooperation.

Winston Churchill's involvement in the Tehran and Yalta Conferences underscored his strategic vision and diplomatic finesse during a crucial period in world history. Simultaneously, his dedication to maintaining the British Empire's unity showcased his commitment to preserving the global influence and cooperation of the Commonwealth nations amid the challenges of wartime. These diplomatic endeavors solidified Churchill's legacy as a statesman capable of navigating the complexities of wartime alliances and envisioning a stable post-war order.

However, the challenges of the post-war era posed a threat to the traditional colonial order. Churchill's vision for the British Empire clashed with the emerging winds of decolonization and self-determination. Despite his best efforts, the post-war world witnessed the gradual dismantling of the empire as former colonies sought independence. His role was nuanced in navigating the complex landscape of post-war geopolitics and empire management. While his wartime leadership had been instrumental, the changing dynamics of the global political stage presented challenges even his statesmanship could not completely overcome.

Winston Churchill's participation in key wartime conferences, like those of Tehran and Yalta, marked crucial junctures in shaping post-war geopolitics. His efforts to maintain the cohesion of the British Empire during this period showcased his commitment to preserving Britain's global influence. However, the winds of change in the post-war era ultimately led to the transformation of the empire, highlighting the complex and evolving nature of Churchill's statesmanship.

1945 Election Loss

This pivotal moment for Churchill shaped his path to the coming events. Although he had amassed a considerable following and made it to the good books of various counterparts, the demographics of politics needed to be simplified.

Political Landscape

The political landscape during the 1945 general election was complex and dynamic. The wartime coalition government, led by Winston Churchill, had been a unique alliance between the Conservative Party and the Labor Party. This arrangement highlighted the necessity of unity in the existential threat posed by the Axis powers. As the war in Europe concluded, though, the political atmosphere transformed. The Labor Party, under the leadership of Clement Attlee, positioned itself as the party with a vision for post-war reconstruction, resonating with a public yearning for change after years of wartime sacrifices.

Public Sentiment

The British public was eager for a new beginning, having endured years of conflict, rationing, and sacrifice. War fatigue influenced public sentiment. There was a palpable desire for leaders who could guide the nation through the transition from wartime challenges to the opportunities and promise of peacetime. The weariness from the prolonged conflict influenced the electorate's receptiveness to messages of change and a fresh start.

Churchill's Wartime Legacy

Winston Churchill's leadership during the war had been extraordinary, and his speeches were emblematic of British resolve and defiance. However, the gratitude for his wartime leadership did not automatically translate into political support for the Conservative Party in the post-war period. While appreciative of Churchill's role during the war, the nation contemplated different skills and priorities for the challenges of reconstruction during a post-war era.

Labor's Vision for Post-War Britain

The Labor Party's manifesto in 1945 presented a comprehensive vision for post-war Britain. This vision included the creation of the National Health Service (NHS) and the establishment of a welfare state. The Labor Party's proposals resonated with a public eager for economic recovery and a fairer and more equitable society. The party positioned itself as the architect of a new, progressive Britain, addressing the social and economic needs of the population.

Changing Demographics

The post-war period witnessed changing demographics, with a younger and more socially conscious electorate coming of age. The desire for social justice and equality became prominent, challenging the more traditional conservative values of Churchill and the Conservative Party. The evolving societal ethos demanded a response from political leaders aligning with the changing expectations and consciousness of the electorate.

Political Realignment

The Labor Party's election campaign in 1945 was effective in portraying itself as the standard-bearers of a new, progressive Britain. Its promises of social reform and transformative policies resonated with voters looking for a fresh direction. The political realignment reflected a broader shift in British politics, with Labor establishing itself as a party capable of winning elections and implementing substantial policy changes.

Cold War Beginnings

The emerging Cold War added a layer of complexity to the political landscape. While Winston Churchill was esteemed for his role in the wartime alliance, the Labor Party was perceived as better equipped to navigate the evolving international tensions. The changing dynamics of the global stage influenced perceptions of which party could effectively manage the challenges of the post-war world, contributing to the Labor Party's electoral success.

Later Return to Power

Winston Churchill's 1945 election loss did not diminish his overall legacy. Despite the defeat, he returned to power as Prime Minister in 1951, proving the nation's enduring respect for his statesmanship and wartime leadership. The complex factors that led to his electoral loss in 1945 highlighted the intricate interplay of historical, political, and societal forces shaping this critical moment in British history.

Chapter 2: The Easy Company Band of Brothers: Brotherhood beyond Battle

The E Company is the 506th Parachute Infantry Regiment of the 101st Airborne Division, popularly known as the *Easy Company*. These paratroopers jumped into direct danger and were pivotal in many key moments of World War II. Their story has been immortalized in the HBO series "Band of Brothers," based on a book written by Stephen E. Ambrose, the founder of the National World War II Museum.

The Easy Company are real-life super soldiers you could only join if you were harder than granite.

The high-flying, elite, and disciplined paratroopers of the E Company took on some of the most dangerous roles in the global conflict. Their heroic missions, where they pulled victories from thin air, even when consistently outgunned and outmanned, were miraculous. Not only were they the first men to storm Normandy so they could open the gates for other troops headed their way via the sea, but they also liberated concentration camps.

The Easy Company are real-life super soldiers you could only join if you were harder than granite. The immensely fit and dedicated division paved the way for paratroopers and used airborne tactics to their advantage. The experimental nature of their missions resulted in some failures, but they powered their way through to become one of the most memorable collectives in the war. The exceptional standards they embraced and their unbridled desire to win are admirable and can be applied to many facets of daily life. The Band of Brothers embodies what it means to continue moving forward even when all the odds are stacked against you. The legendary Easy Company stands tall as the bravest of the brave, emerging as a shining example of pure toughness.

D-Day Jump at Normandy

On June 6, 1944, the Allied forces collaborated in one of the biggest invasions in history. Nazi Germany was controlling France and fighting the Soviets on the Eastern Front. The Allies realized that the German forces were spread too thin and couldn't send reinforcements to the beach bases on the coastline of France. British and Canadian soldiers captured the beaches codenamed Gold, Juno, and Sword, while the Americans captured Omaha and Utah. The most resistance the Allied forces encountered was at Omaha. Despite that, they were successful. The Allied forces lost about 4,000 men out of the 156,000 troops. The successful invasion allowed the Allies to set up a port to send through an additional 326,000 troops, 50,000 military vehicles, and over 100,000 tons of much-needed equipment. The storming of Normandy Beach opened a chain reaction that would allow the Allies to push into Europe through France, eventually obtaining the unconditional surrender of Nazi Germany.

The Easy Company of the 2nd Battalion, 506th parachute infantry regiment, joined the 101st Airborne Division to fulfill a unique role in the storming of Normandy. The brave troopers parachuted behind enemy lines near Utah Beach on the Cotentin peninsula. They blocked key causeways so the U.S. 4th Infantry Division could freely push out of Utah Beach further into France. The "Screaming Eagles," nicknamed because of the eagle insignia on their uniforms, opened the way for the amphibious invasion of Normandy. They were the first soldiers to set foot into France on that historic turn in the war.

The division leaped into the unknown, suffering many losses along the way. Leaders were skeptical about the experimental unit, with British Prime Minister Winston Churchill and the Allied Head, General Dwight Eisenhower, scrutinizing whether the unit could be successful. Many top generals predicted that the paratroopers would suffer 80% casualties. Their fears were slightly confirmed when, during demonstrations, a man lost his life, and 10% of the division was hospitalized. During the training period, troops had to complete five solo jumps before joining the division and receiving their wings. Since the division was entirely made up of volunteers, receiving this certification was considered a significant honor.

The training to be a Screaming Eagle was intense, with only one in three applicants making it through. They were trained to be a one-man army that was tough as nails and could push their way through enemy forces alone when they landed and later united with their team. The incentive to join the 101st Airborne Division was substantial because they received a $50 jumping bonus, bumped up to $100 if you were an officer. Some soldiers joked that they unknowingly accepted blood money in bonuses when they signed up.

By the time June 1934 rolled around, the Screaming Eagles were in England, well aware of their orders to parachute into Normandy and clear the way for the sea forces that would follow them. They prepared for their jump with a ceremonial last meal of pork chops and fried chicken, which the troops thoroughly enjoyed. As they boarded the plane, the reality of their task hit every soldier bowing down his head to say his silent prayer of protection and guidance. Eisenhower's concern was shown until the last minute when he arrived to see the men off. In an emotional display of genuine empathy, he did not give a rallying speech but approached each soldier and wished them luck. As the planes took off, he silently saluted the courageous men, many of whom would die during their mission. As they flew over the 6000 vessels approaching the beaches of Normandy, off the shores of England, the gravity of their role hit them like a ton of bricks.

General Maxwell D. Taylor promised the men that they only needed to fight with all their might for three solid days, and they would earn their release. However, he could not keep his promise because they eventually completed their mission about a month later. Disaster struck as soon as they entered French air space occupied by the Germans. Anti-aircraft weapons ripped their planes to shreds. The heavy fire forced the pilots to abandon their orders and break the formation. Instead of jumping at 700ft at 100 miles per hour, they had to jump at 300ft at 200 miles per hour. At that high speed, the winds tore through their parachutes, causing them to land with minimal weapons to fight the well-armed Nazis. Some troops landed in the water and drowned, while others, unfortunately, fell right into the enemy's lap and were killed as soon as their feet touched the ground.

In the division's first mission, they applied their strenuous training to get the job done in adverse circumstances. Being chaotically scattered ironically worked in their favor because the Germans couldn't identify a clear frontline. The Screaming Eagles were explicitly trained for guerilla conditions and to fight in small units. Furthermore, landing in random places allowed many troops to gather valuable intelligence. The makeshift units overwhelmed the German military, unprepared for this scattered fighting style. The 101st Airborne Division had some tricks up their sleeves. They used a children's "cricket" toy to identify one another. A trooper would click the toy once and get a response of two clicks. This easy-to-remember code proved invaluable in the heat of battle. Their extensive preparation made them unstoppable against a bewildered German force on the beaches of Normandy.

Operation Market Garden

Following the Normandy invasion in June 1944, the Allied forces embarked on their most extensive operation during WWII. The E Company joined Operation Market Garden. Their role was to parachute into the Netherlands and take over the strategic bridges at the Waal, Lower Rhine, and Meuse rivers, which the Germans controlled. The airborne mission aimed for paratroopers to enter and hold the bridges until ground forces arrived. If the plan was successfully executed, it was likely that the Allied forces would be victorious by Christmas of the same year. However, the operation resulted in one of the greatest failures of the Allied forces.

Even though they succeeded initially, a few factors worked against the paratroopers. Firstly, most of the men landed where they had planned precisely, which allowed the Germans to assess the company's strategic goals according to their location. Secondly, since they could only carry light weaponry, the paratroopers underestimated how long they could hold the bridges until their infantrymen arrived. Thirdly, the Allied aircraft were not big enough to deliver the number of troops needed for the operation, so they dropped them off in intervals, allowing the Germans to predict where they were landing and eliminating the element of surprise. Lastly, the time to plan such an elaborate operation was simply not enough to achieve their lofty goals. General Walter Bedell Smith warned Montgomery about the sizeable German presence in the Netherlands, but he ignored the warnings and stubbornly proceeded with his flawed plan.

Operation Market Garden was the brainchild of Field Marshal Sir Bernard Law Montgomery. The Allies, up until this point, had used a broad approach to reach the German frontier. However, Montgomery feared that their slow advance would require constant supplies, and they were allowing the Germans to better their defenses. Montgomery proposed to General Eisenhower that they should opt for a more direct approach to get them to the German front much faster and with fewer resources being expended.

Operation Market Garden would deviate from the broad approach to end the war quickly, opting for a narrow thrust through the Netherlands to avoid the German Siegfried line's defenses. The Easy Company's paratroopers were meant to drop into the Netherlands to secure bridges over the canal in Eindhoven, Nijmegen, and Arnhem. With these bridges secured, the British XXX Corps would have a clear path into Ruhr, the industrial hub of the German war machine.

The plan went south when the U.S. 82nd Airborne Division fought the Germans at the Nijmegen Bridge. The British XXX Corps provided support and, after a long and tedious battle, eventually won the bridge to cross the River Waal. At Arnhem, there was massive resistance that the Allied Forces could not break. Crossing the River Waal was useless because they were in no position to fight the well-equipped German forces after the battle at Nijmegen. They had to pull out of the region and abandon the ill-fated plan. This was the last victory the Nazis would have against the Allies.

Defense of Bastogne

The Battle of the Ardennes was the last large German offensive against the Allied forces. The attack was a desperate attempt to separate the American and British Forces. This would void the need for an unconditional and give the Germans negotiating power with each side while they continued fighting the Soviets on the Eastern Front. The Battle of the Bulge, as it was later called, lasted about six weeks after commencing on December 16, 1944. A 200,000-strong German army and 1,000 tanks approached the Americans in the Ardennes forest. Poor visibility caused by bad weather meant the Allied Air Forces could not assist. Many units were forced to surrender on the first day of the attack, while some took a defensive position at Bastogne.

The Nazi forces were unaware of the cloth the Easy Company was cut from. Even though the company was surrounded, they were unwilling to give up. With their ammunition quickly running low and food supplies almost depleted, the Easy Company continued to fight the Germans bravely. Besides their dwindling supplies, they suffered in the freezing cold. However, despite their extreme fatigue, they held off the Germans for seven bitter days.

The Germans did not know how close they were to defeating the 101st Airborne Division. The Screaming Eagles set their defensive position around the Bastogne area because they assumed they were surrounded by Germans. However, they couldn't be sure because of the low visibility conditions. The Nazi forces attacked them in short bursts with smaller units, a fighting style that favored the skillset of the Screaming Eagles. If the Germans had attacked them with the entirety of their forces at once, the 101st would most likely have lost. Therefore, the Germans' miscalculation and one terrible plan handed the victory to the 101st.

The Germans were running low on fuel and unable to navigate the dense forest swiftly enough to facilitate the constant bombardment needed for the win. Moreover, the muddy conditions affected the mobility of their tanks. Since the weather and supply availability were also not going in the favor of the Nazis, the Screaming Eagles held them off while suffering heavy casualties. Eventually, the Third Army contacted the 101st Division and relieved them of their duty. Once the weather cleared, they could get more supplies, and the wounded soldiers were treated.

Since the 101st Division was no longer surrounded, they could expand and recapture the villages they had been forced to abandon during the initial siege. The Third Army claimed they saved the 101st Division from complete destruction. But if you were to ask one of the hardened members of the unit, you'd never get them to admit such a thing. The unrelenting Screaming Eagles courageously defended against a last-ditch effort of the Germans to gain an advantage on the Western Front. After this attack, Hitler's house of cards quickly fell. The Germans would lose every battle against the Allies following the Ardennes siege, leading to the Allies' ultimate victory and the end of the war.

Liberation of Concentration Camps

One of the most horrific and brutal terrors of the Nazi regime was the concentration camps. When thinking about concentration camps, people typically envision industrialized death with millions of Jewish people being gassed. There were camps where people were tortured and starved while Nazi scientists conducted dehumanizing experiments on them. The torture and death that took place in concentration camps is why the Holocaust is remembered as the single greatest atrocity to ever happen to a group of people.

The Easy Company was reminded of what they were fighting for when the 101st Division and the 12th Armored Division discovered the Kaufering concentration camp in Landsberg in April 1945. Both units first encountered Kaufering IV, one of eleven camps making up the complex. Before they arrived, the SS marched the prisoners out to their deaths and burned down the barracks. The camp could hold 3,600 prisoners in horrendous conditions. When the units arrived, many of the inhabitants had died, and others were too weak to move. The soldiers ordered the locals to make sure the dead were buried.

The 82nd Airborne Division liberated the Wöbbelin camp about a month later in the city of Ludwigslust. This disease-ridden camp was even bigger than the one discovered at Kaufering, with about 5,000 malnourished prisoners. 1,000 prisoners were buried with the Star of David placed on the graves of the Jewish deceased and a cross on the graves of Christians. The limited food and water at the camp resulted in captives resorting to cannibalism. These camps traumatized the Easy Company but reignited their drive to bring an end to the war.

Post-War and Legacy

The Eagle will always scream for our fallen brothers

Name	Service #	Date
John T. Julian	34806849	01/45
Warren H. Muck	12131169	01/45
Alex M. Penkala	35549002	01/45
Carl C. Sawosko	16100548	01/45
John E. Shindell	35530711	01/45
Harold D. Webb	35880340	01/45
Kenneth J. Webb	32383307	01/45
Harold G. Hayes	34892610	12/44
Donald B. Hoobler	20508303	01/45
Francis J. Mellett	20229437	01/45
A.P. Herron	33657700	01/45
Patrick H. Neill	12238576	01/45
Richard J. Hughes	42104549	01/45
Eugene E. Jackson	13011296	12/44

Many individuals of the Easy Company's names will forever be lost to the archives of history.
https://commons.wikimedia.org/wiki/File:Easy_company_foy03.jpg

Many individuals of the Easy Company's names will forever be lost to the archives of history. The blood they spilled is all the honor they will receive for their heroic efforts. The legacy of the Easy Company is perseverance in the face of unfavorable odds. A few key members' lives and how they fared after the war were detailed in the Band of Brothers miniseries. Major Winters became a successful businessman working at Nixon Nitration Works. He was reinstated during the Korean War but never saw combat. He helped Stephen Ambrose with writing for "Band of Brothers."

Edward Heffron tried to save his comrade John T. Julian. He ran through enemy fire, but unfortunately, he did not manage to save his close friend. His actions were indicative of the attitudes of the incredible people of the Easy Company. Heffron describes how he hates New Year's Day because it reminds him of the war and the tragic loss of his friend. Ronald Speirs, who valiantly fought in the Battle of the Bulge, remained in the U.S. Army after the war. He retired in 1964 after 22 years. He fought against the North Koreans as a paratrooper as well. He was also deployed in Laos during the country's civil war and as a liaison officer to the Soviet Union in East Germany. His final call to duty was as a plans officer for the Pentagon.

Darrell Powers, a skilled sniper for the Company, worked as a machinist in California after a car accident he was involved in. He suffered from health and mental issues later in his life, eventually succumbing to lung cancer at the age of 86. He married Dorothy, the love of his life, and they lived together for 60 years until his death. Herbert Sobel's life after the war was tragic. He divorced his wife Rose and attempted suicide, but the bullet did not kill him. Instead, it blinded him. He died of malnutrition in 1987, and no funeral was held to honor his memory. Lewis Nixon III, who was part of the D-Day invasion, Operation Market Garden, and the Battle of the Bulge, retired to a life of relative ease. He died from diabetes complications. William "Wild Bill" Guarnere, the loose cannon of the bunch who always put himself in harm's way, lost his leg to a war injury. He died at the old age of 90.

Chapter 3: Irena Sendler: The Warsaw Ghetto's Guardian Angel

"My father instilled in me two principles: People are good or bad, and religion, race, and nationality are immaterial. What counts is the distinction between good and bad." Irena Sendler

A woman who went out of her way to save and protect those with whom she did not share any relation aside from being of the same species.

It is said that those who endure and survive warfare are forever scarred by its dark, long talons. It is no secret that war brings out the best and worst in humans. When faced with survival moments, you could choose a route you never thought possible, putting yourself before those you love the most and making decisions that may go against your current values or morals. However, this is not the story of this chapter's heroine. A woman who went out of her way to save and protect those with whom she did not share any relation aside from being of the same species.

Irena Sendler was born in an era when women were expected to run and hide. She existed at the center of a raging conflict between the oppressor and the oppressed. She chose to be on the right side of history. Shedding away her fears and concerns for her safety, she left an everlasting mark, proving that humans can be good to one another regardless of their ethnic differences.

Sendler was born to a catholic family on February 15, 1910, in Otwock, Poland, a resort town near Warsaw. Before World War II, the small town was often frequented by Jews. Irena grew up watching her catholic father's kind and sympathetic dealings with their Jewish neighbors, instilling in her the notion that all people are born equal. As a child, she made it a habit to play with the Jewish children, which was uncommon for a Catholic child.

Her father, Dr. Stanislaw Krzyzanowski, one of the few doctors who had no reservations about treating Jews, had a famous saying, "Jump into the water to save someone drowning, whether or not you can swim." Irena took those words to heart, growing up to become a champion of social justice, hell-bent on rescuing the Jews from the Nazi occupation.

Irena studied Law and Polish studies at the University of Warsaw, where she did not shy away from condemning and protesting against the discrimination of the Jews. Irena joined the leftist Union of Polish Democratic Youth.

At the dawn of the 1930s, Irena worked at the Mother and Child Assistance Division in the legal department. The division was part of the Free Polish University, Wolna Wszechnica Polska. In 1935, she worked at the Warsaw Department of Social Welfare and Public Health in Warsaw as a social worker, which was known for aiding Jews and Christians suffering from dire circumstances in the city. Her main duties within the organization were focused on guiding and helping young, homeless women and single mothers. She'd offer them advice, including how to prevent sexual infections or illnesses and safeguard against unwanted pregnancies.

The German Invasion

A dark cloud descended upon Poland and the Jews in particular when Germany bested the Poles in battle and occupied Warsaw in September 1939. The Germans' values differed quite drastically from Irena's. They were more concerned with enslaving, humiliating, terrorizing, and slaughtering those whom they deemed inferior to them. In other words, the Jews.

Irena, a 29-year-old social worker at the time of the occupation, was more than eager to lend a helping hand to the ill-treated Jews. Together with her friends, Jadwiga Piotrowska, Irena Schultz, and Jadwiga Deneko, they used their positions to provide as much monetary and physical assistance to their Jewish community as they could.

The Nazis imposed an ironclad dictatorship, forcing the Jews to live in concentration camps or ghettos in 1940. The Jews in these ghettos were subjected to inhumane circumstances regarding medical and basic living needs. The Nazis would often move the Jews from the ghettos to death or extermination camps (Treblinka death camp), where they met their demise. This action was known as "the great liquidation action." If a Jew attempted to escape the walls of the ghetto, it subjected them to an immediate death penalty.

The Warsaw Ghetto was one of the largest Jewish concentration camps in Europe, with over 400,000 confined Jews. It was a small area where the Jews were placed and separated from the remaining Christian population with high walls and barbed wires.

Any attempts made by the Polish Christians to help alleviate the distressing circumstances of their Jewish friends were met with violent repercussions from the German soldiers. These consequences usually meant the loss of life.

As the Nazis' intentions to wipe out the Jewish race became clear, the Poles realized that the aid provided to their friends had to be well organized and carefully planned for it to work.

Sendler had access to enter the Warsaw Ghetto using permits from the Department of Sanitization. The Germans often allowed social workers to enter out of fear that an outbreak of Typhus within the camp would travel beyond its walls and harm those on the outside. Sendler witnessed the atrocities and horrendous conditions the Jews were subjected to every time she entered the Ghetto. People were waiting to be transferred to the death camps to meet their imminent death or dying from hunger and disease caused by having a huge number of people in such a small area.

Using her access and her colleagues' support in the organization, as many as 3,000 Jews, men, women, and children received aid, such as food, money, and medicine. Within the ghetto, Irena used the code name Klara.

Irena would smuggle the Jewish children out of the Ghetto with the help of her colleagues from the Welfare Department and lead them to the so-called "Aryan Side."

The children were often placed with Christian families or within care facilities. They were given fake identities to hide from the German invaders and the complicit Polish citizens who denounced the Jews.

The Zegota Council

In December of 1942, the Zegota was established. The Zegota was a code name for the council created by the Poles to support the Jewish community. The council was led by Chairman Julian Grobelny, who went by the code name Trojan.

Sendler was a leading member of the Zegota council and went by the code name Jolanta. She was one of many social activists who undertook dangerous and life-threatening missions to rescue as many Jews as possible.

The council had many duties, including providing food, shelter, clothes, and money and forging documents for the Jews to pass undetected under the German noses. The Jews were often coached in Christian masses and mannerisms so they could pass as devout Christians instead of Jews.

The council agreed that Sendler should lead the children's bureau within the organization. Irena had a talent for outmaneuvering the Germans with her experience working as a social worker. She was in charge of the network that transferred money and sought safe hiding places for the rescued children. The team employed several methods to move the young children out of the ghetto undetected.

The children were smuggled in the most creative ways. They were hidden in medical bags, coffins, body bags, parcels, gunny sacks, and secret compartments within ambulances. Five-month-old Elzbieta Ficowska was carried out in a toolbox.

The rescuers sometimes used the corridors and gates of the Polish court since its doors opened to the Polish side of the street out of the ghetto. However, their success usually depended on the kind hearts of the Polish janitors facilitating their movements through the building.

A more challenging rescue route was linking the basements within the ghetto and the basements on the Polish side through a maze of underground tunnels. A simpler way took advantage of one Zegota member as a tram operator. Sendler or one of her associates would falsify documents for the Jewish child in case they were stopped by a German soldier. The child would then be taken to the tram that crossed over to the Polish side.

No avenues were left unexplored when it came to saving the children. However, it cannot be a heroic story without melancholy. The children's parents were understandably reluctant to part with their loved ones. They asked for guarantees that their child would survive the journey or outright refuse to give them up. Sendler and her friends tried to remain as honest as possible, stating that they couldn't provide a guarantee that they, themselves, would leave the ghetto alive. All they could do was try.

Safe Houses

The children's bureau found catholic houses that volunteered to care for the children as their own or place the young victims in private homes. But the Polish clergy took a major hit when the Nazis occupied Poland. Many priests, monks, and nuns lost their lives helping the Jews.

The catholic priests worked with the Zegota community to provide a safe haven to the distressed young, away from the claws of the Germans. They performed baptisms and provided fake certificates to some survivors to fool the Germans into thinking they were Christians. Many monastic organizations were ready to help the displaced Jews. These organizations included the Mission (Vincentians) congregation, the Salesian Society, the Association of Catholic Apostleship, and many more.

Father Jozef Pochoda, a Parish Priest, was one of the lucky survivors who escaped the Gestapo after they discovered he had baptized 2 Jewish children. Typically, the children moved from one religious institution to another to avoid being caught.

Father Boduen's Home was a famous destination for the displaced children. Around 220 Jewish children were placed there by the Guardian Angel of Warsaw and her companions. Even though many Polish citizens were privy to the knowledge of Jewish children residing in his home, no one ratted them out to the Gestapo. In many cases, the home of Rev. Boduen only served as a transitional phase for the child to get to safety. Before the child's extraction, data would be provided by phone detailing the exact arrival time and the child's features and appearance.

The nun convents were the best places to care for the children due to their placement in remote areas away from the eyes of the German Nazis. Nuns believed it to be their sacred duty to care for the children affected by the terror of war.

An arrangement was struck between Sendler and the nuns of 4 major orders (the Grey Sisters, the Little Servants of the Immaculate Conception, the Franciscans of the Family of Mary, and the Order of Saint Elizabeth). Upon receiving a specific code word, the nuns traveled to Warsaw, collected the Jewish boys and girls, and returned with them to their convents for safekeeping.

Many Polish families volunteered to care for the children once their forged documents were produced. More often than not, the families were childless couples looking for a child to complete their family. The children were mostly too young to understand the dilemma they were caught in, so they quickly got used to their new caretakers. However, the older children found it more challenging to adapt to the changed environment, as they lived in terror of the imminent danger of being identified as a Jew and eventually killed.

Sendler kept a record on a narrow strip of tissue paper with the details of every rescued child, their Jewish names, temporary catholic names, and where they were placed. This list served as a hope that one day when the war was over, the children would be reunited with their biological families. Many of these lists were hidden in jars and buried under an apple tree near the German barracks.

Irena Sendler's Capture

The Gestapo had a growing suspicion about Irena's actions. On October 20, 1943, they raided her apartment to search for evidence. At the time, Irena was with her sick mother and another friend who was sister-in-arms in their rescue missions. Out of fear for the saved children being discovered, Irena handed the index with the Jewish names to her friend, who tucked it into her underwear before the Gestapo entered. The Gestapo went through the entire apartment searching for incriminating evidence for 2 long hours but to no avail.

Disgruntled with their lack of findings, the Gestapo apprehended Irena and escorted her to Pawiak, a prison where many Polish people met their demise at the hands of the Nazis. Sendler was subjected to beatings, torment, and violation in many forms. They broke her legs and feet during interrogations to force her into confessing, but she stood her ground and remained silent. She was sentenced to death and led to believe that her time on this earth was up. Nonetheless, her good deeds caught up to her, and Zegota member Maria Palester arranged a bribe to break her out of confinement. Her daughter Malgosia made the payment, hidden in her bag beneath noodles and porridge.

Following her release, Irena took on a new identity and went underground. Following her recovery, Irena Sendler continued her work with Zegota, rescuing and placing children in safe homes until the Warsaw uprising in August-September 1944. Sendler stayed with the Palesters, who helped free her from prison and worked as a nurse on Falata Street in a medical aid unit.

The End of the War

Following the war's end, Irena dug up the jars with the index of names of the Jewish children rescued to attempt to find their parents and reunite the broken families. She handed the information to a representative of the Jewish committee. Unfortunately, after much inspection and thorough searches, it was determined that most of the parents of the displaced children were killed in the Treblinka death camp.

Irena didn't stop her selfless work after Poland's liberation. She dove head first into several projects to help the needy and vulnerable. She put together orphanages and worked with her colleagues to establish nursing homes and several other social welfare institutions. She later joined the Polish United Workers Party.

Irena had 3 children (2 boys and a girl) with her second husband, Adam Celnikier, whom she helped in the ghetto. Before the end of the war, they lived together under the name Zgrzembski to avoid the Gestapo's prying eyes. One of her sons passed away after birth. The other died in the 1990s from heart disease. In the aftermath of the war, Irena wasn't granted the proper recognition by the Polish government for her efforts.

Sendler fell ill in 1968 and stopped working. Around the same time, the anti-Semitic campaign was born in Poland, leading several thousands of Jews to flee the country. Irena was appalled by the injustice that the Jews continued to suffer and suggested to her old war colleague, Jadwiga Piotrowska, to create a new Zegota.

Irena lived in anonymity until her story was made known around the 2000s. It is said that a teacher called Norman Conrad, in 1999, showed his students in Kansas a clipping from a magazine about the woman who saved 2500 Jewish children during the holocaust. He assigned his students the task of finding who she was and the extraordinary story behind such a feat. Four of his students accepted his challenge, did their research, and wrote a play called "Life in a Jar" as a tribute to the index Irena hid in jars under the apple tree.

The story told by the 4 students shed an overdue light on the story of the Guardian Angel of Warsaw, who defied the odds and challenged the German Nazis. The play was later turned into a feature film and performed over 200 times on stage. As a direct result of her story becoming known, Irena was granted many awards, the highest of which was a candidacy for a Nobel Peace Prize in 2008. In 2003, she was awarded the Jan Karski Award for valor and courage. She also received the Order of the White Eagle. Another award she received is the "Order of the Smile," which is usually presented by children. Sendler stated that the award was one of the nicest recognitions she received. Part of the tradition entails that the award recipient must drink lemon juice and smile before it's handed to them.

Irena Sendler passed away on May 12, 2008. Since then, her life has been celebrated by many in different forms. Her name is on streets, squares, and schools, and her picture decorates murals, stamps, and coins.

Irena's courage during WWII stands as a testament to the selfless nature of her life. Her memory continues to inspire and guide those who seek light in the face of overwhelming darkness. She was a woman who defied the odds and took action when the most common action at the time was inaction.

Chapter 4: The Navajo Code Talkers: Heroes of the Pacific

With the onset of WWII, military forces across the globe realized the importance of structured scientific research and development, especially in communications electronics. Revolutionary advancements that allowed transnational real-time communications, improvements in wire and radio transmission systems, enhanced navigation aids, and other innovations meant that military forces had to improve their code development and interpretation.

The Navajo and the entire Native American community faced adversities and prejudices despite their intelligence and efforts during the war.

This chapter explores the critical need for a secure communication system in the Pacific Theater, setting the stage for the Navajo Code Talkers, the heroic code makers. You'll gain insight into the advancements made during the war and why they required better code development and interpretation skills. You'll also learn how the Navajo language, unwritten and barely unknown outside the Navajo community, contributed to the Allies' victory. The chapter delves into the adversities and prejudices the Navajo and the entire Native American community faced despite their intelligence and efforts during the war. Reading this chapter, you'll discover why the contributions of the Navajo Code Talkers were kept secret for decades after the war and how they finally received their well-deserved recognition and commendation.

The Need for Communication Systems: Technology and Code

Real-Time Radio Communications

During WWII, military forces realized the need for communication equipment to transmit high-quality, real-time information in large quantities. Their needs were far beyond the technological capabilities of the industry at the time. Forces needed to develop innovative and highly effective methods of communication, so improved research and development departments specializing in communications-electronics and manufacturing plants were sought. At that time, radio transmissions were also paramount.

Several departments within the army, such as air forces, armored teams, artillery forces, and infantry personnel, prompted the need for real-time radio communications. Upon the development of the technology, each individual in the military, regardless of their rank, was provided at least one radio. Depending on their position in the military hierarchy and assigned role, some were given up to 3 radios. They relied on wired communication, characterized by its quick and highly adaptable nature. Multiconductor cables supported up to 4 conversations and were first adopted by the Germans.

Revolutionary Advancements

Many people don't know that World War II drove groundbreaking scientific and technological advancements that shape life today. From microwaves to radar technologies, wartime advancements made their way into daily post-war civilian life. For instance, radar technology is now integral to meteorology and accurate weather-detection capabilities. The progression of more powerful computers during the war led to the creation of the first general-purpose computers, marking a transformative moment in the world's history and the emergence of a new era of transcontinental communications.

Medical advancements made during the war, like the increased production of penicillin and antibiotics as treatments for bacterial infections, were turning points in medicine. Several surgical and trauma treatment innovations also emerged. These outstanding medical headways continuously allow medical professionals to save countless lives every day.

The atomic bomb is perhaps the most famous advancement of all due to its capability to wreak havoc and define outcomes during wartime. Its use in World War II marked the onset of the atomic age and triggered a never-ending nuclear arms race between the Soviet Union and the U.S. The two nations engaged in a geopolitical, space-related race, essentially leading to the creation of NASA and the moon landing in 1969. These events influenced diplomacy, shaped world politics, and shaped the size and power of military forces. They also served as a stepping stone for future scientific and technological advancements.

Several new and highly refined communication devices were also developed as the war progressed. The "Loran," one of the newest electronic advancements, was used for long-range electronic navigation, which was useful for aircraft and naval vessels. The "Shoran" was for short-range navigational systems.

Aircraft landing systems witnessed significant improvements. Engineers combined their knowledge of communications and radars to streamline the aircraft landing process, even when the pilot's line of sight was blocked entirely. The "ground-controlled approach system," GCA, was the most popular aircraft landing control guide.

Another system known as GCI, "ground-controlled intercept," was also developed. This system comprised combinations of radar, communication, and radio direction-finding technologies. The GCI was curated to aid with the ground control of interceptors.

Radio-controlled bomb guidance was another key advancement because it allowed bomb operators to direct bombs to their intended targets accurately. Electronic countermeasures were introduced, allowing forces to disrupt radio channels, navigation, radar, and other systems.

The Need for Unbreakable Code

The advancement of wartime communication technologies meant that military forces had to improve their code development and interpretation. Wireless radio communications became extremely widespread, putting top-secret information at risk of interception. Sensitive plans and orders were transmitted through wireless radios, so armies had to get creative with their secret codes. They needed to ensure no one other than trained personnel caught onto these messages.

Enigma Code and ULTRA Intelligence

The Polish and British were very successful at deciphering German messages transmitted in the Enigma code. In addition to their excellent cryptography skills, they could easily pick up on the patterns with the help of a German traitor. The Germans initially had no idea their enemies deciphered their messages. However, they suspected something was wrong when they could no longer effectively sink as many enemy ships as before. The German Navy refined their Enigma machines, specialized encryption devices, to salvage the situation, allowing them to better target and sink enemy ships once again.

PURPLE Code and MAGIC Intelligence

The Japanese didn't have cryptographic systems as sophisticated as the Germans, making them prone to interpretation. The U.S. army and navy successfully deciphered diplomatic messages that went back and forth between Tokyo and Japanese embassies in Berlin, London, Rome, Washington, and other areas. However, for the most part, their efforts went to waste. While the Japanese code PURPLE was entirely deciphered using intelligence gathered from the interpreted MAGIC code, it didn't explicitly mention any military plans. Hence, the U.S. didn't anticipate the attack on Pearl Harbor.

As the war progressed, the U.S. and the Allied forces used MAGIC and ULTRA to decrypt German Enigma machine-encrypted messages to stay ahead of their enemies. Even though code PURPLE didn't offer a prior warning about the Pearl Harbor attack, Japanese communications provided extremely important information about the production of Nazi weapons and Germany's aim to protect Europe. They also learned that Japan wouldn't surrender and maintain its position unless forced or significantly pressured to do otherwise.

The U.S. and the Allies, especially the British Royal Navy, used a wide array of techniques to decipher secret codes transmitted across the Germans and Japanese. Most notably, they got their hands on extremely valuable codebooks that helped them interpret the codes. In 1940, the British Navy captured a German ship. During the attack, the Germans tried to get rid of the books by throwing them into the ocean. The Allies recovered a substantial portion of the codebook, though, granting them insight into German codes and information.

In 1942, British sailors retrieved an even larger portion of German codebooks when they were found on a sinking German U-boat in the Mediterranean Ocean. Two British sailors died during this mission, and the recovered codebooks were vital for Allied cryptanalysts. It was the code the Germans used to communicate across their submarines. By the end of 1942, the U.S. and the Allies decoded up to 4,000 German messages a day, allowing them to effectively counter attacks led by the enemy.

Cryptologists often had to sift through millions of different possibilities until they landed at the right solutions using their incredible mathematical skills and computer expertise. The study of cryptology saved countless lives during the war, contributed to the Allies' victory, and significantly cut the war's duration. Field professionals suggest that if it weren't for the diligent code-breaking efforts, the war could've resumed for an estimated additional two years.

The Navajo Code Talkers

In the early 1940s, the United States Marine Corps developed a program that would allow them to conduct secure and effective communication, the Navajo Code Talkers. The Navajo are the largest federally recognized tribe in the nation. This Native American group inhabits the Southwestern region of the United States. The Marines recruited 29 Navajo men who used their native language to create an unbreakable code to deliver sensitive messages and information during the war.

The Navajo team partook in the attacks the Marine Corps led until 1945. This was a genius move because the enemy never deciphered the code even though they transmitted messages back and forth through radios and telephones, which the Japanese easily accessed. Japan was notorious for breaking messages and military codes transmitted across the Pacific, making it extremely challenging to strategize and maintain the surprise and sensitive elements of war.

The Creation of the Navajo Code Talkers Program

Philip Johnston, a veteran of the First World War, was the mastermind behind the Navajo Code Talkers program. He was inspired by an article about how the army had previously used Native American soldiers for similar purposes. He recruited Navajo men in particular because his father was a missionary who lived in the Navajo Nation. He was already familiar with the culture and language and was confident the language would be difficult to decipher. At the time, not even the surrounding tribes understood Navajo.

His background and experience allowed him to present a solid pitch to Major James E. Jones. While Major Jones initially doubted the idea's effectiveness, Johnston easily convinced him once he started speaking in Navajo. Major Jones instructed him to proceed with the Navajo people right away.

Johnston's test run with the Navajo men proved to be highly successful. Initially, the language had no writing system until missionaries arrived in the region and created an alphabet. The language's complexity and lack of existence in writing made it very promising for military code purposes. On February 28, 1942, four Navajo men demonstrated how they could send and receive messages coded in the Navajo language. A few days later, Major Gen. Clayton B. Vogel signed a letter portraying his favorable attitude toward recruiting 200 Navajo men in the Marine Corps.

While the initial enlistment of the native men was approved, there were additional standard requirements the men had to meet to be officially recruited, such as age, health, and citizenship qualifications. The candidates had to undergo a 7-week training program. They went through basic military training, improved their English and Navajo communication skills, developed and memorized certain Navajo-based codes, learned to use specific equipment, completed rigorous military training, and taught security protocol. Of the numerous candidates, 29 Navajo recruits developed the code and served in the military. Over 400 Navajo men eventually joined the program and served in different divisions of the Marines.

The Development of the Navajo Code

The idea of the code was fairly easy. The men had to choose words from the Navajo language and apply each to common military phrases. The code was initially made of 211 Navajo terms. However, as the program's success became evident, the code was expanded to feature 411 terms. Another factor that made the code so hard to decipher was that the Navajo language didn't have military terminology. The developers had to create new Navajo terms and assign them meanings. For instance, the Navajo language didn't have a word for "ship." Therefore, the men combined the Navajo words meaning "Sea" and "Force," granting the new meaning of "ship." Navajo terms like "bird carrier" and "iron fish" were also used to reference English words like "aircraft" and "submarine."

To further complicate things for the enemy, the Navajo Code Talkers created a Navajo alphabet system where each of the English alphabet's 26 letters corresponded to a Navajo word. They used this unique system to write and send messages in English that would be impossible to decipher. They had everything memorized and didn't leave any traces of written evidence of the code. They later expanded the alphabet to 44 letters when they realized some letters in English were used very frequently. They wanted to avoid the risk of the enemy catching on to the theory behind or parts of the code.

The Japanese captured Navajo Sergeant J0e Kieyoomia and were certain he knew the key to deciphering the code and tortured him so he would eventually crack under pressure. However, even though Kieyoomia spoke Navajo, he was never trained to decipher the code. The encrypted messages sounded like an indiscernible mess of disorganized words to him. The code developers thought of every detail. They made sure no one, not even those fluent in Navajo, could ever decipher the code if they weren't trained!

The Navajo code was a fast and highly secure means of communication - existing methods required around 30 minutes to decode 3 lines of English using code-breaking machines. The Code Talkers translated the same number of words in only 20 seconds. Since they memorized the code, the Code Talkers had to decipher each message in real time using only their memory. The development process was well-thought-out, leaving no room for error. For instance, during the battle of Iwo Jima, only 6 Code Talkers were involved in translating over

800 messages across the frontlines.

The process was done seamlessly, and all messages were sent, transmitted, delivered, and decoded without errors. While the code was highly adaptable to suit various communications, the code talkers avoided writing the code down and only communicated through radio and telephone. The intensive training program ensured that the Code Talkers effectively transmitted and deciphered messages, even under intense war conditions.

Around 15 of the original Code Talkers joined the first Marines division as they planned the attack in the Pacific arena at Guadalcanal. They were officially enlisted only when they had proved successful on the battlefield.

Challenges and Discrimination

The Code Talkers played an indispensable role during the war. Major Howard Connor explained that the battle of Iwo Jima would've never been an American success if it hadn't been for the Navajos. Despite their contributions, like all Native Americans at the time, the Navajo Code Talkers were widely discriminated against. This prejudice not only occurred before the war but also took place during and after, while they worked tirelessly to achieve American victory.

Many Native American children were forcefully enrolled in governmental boarding schools and required to abandon their native languages and speak English. Chester Nez, one of the initial Code Talkers, once mentioned that he was frustrated that after years of forcing him and his people to speak only English, the government asked for their help to use the same language they were asked to abandon.

The Navajo people were not allowed to vote in Arizona until 3 years after the war. Five years later, in 1953, they were granted voting rights in New Mexico. Utah followed 2 years later. Their lack of voting rights was a prevailing problem even though the 1924 Snyder Act was signed granting U.S. citizenship to all U.S.-born Native Americans. However, the discrimination went far beyond the inability to vote. Native Americans were often denied service at, or even entrance to, restaurants, hotels, and other public services outside the Navajo nation. Although the Code Talkers were war veterans, they had no access to numerous veteran benefits.

Post-War Secrecy and Anticipated Recognition

Even though they deserved recognition and distinction for their efforts, the Code Talkers were hidden from the public eye. The Navajo Code Talker program remained highly classified until 1968, when new Code deciphering methods emerged, deeming the program obsolete. They weren't welcomed home with praise or celebrations as details regarding the program and knowledge of its existence were kept secret decades after the war. It wasn't until 1982 that President Ronald Reagan announced August 14 as National Code Talkers Day. In 2001, the 29 initial Code Talkers were recognized for their contributions and successes. The U.S. government officially awarded them the Congressional Gold Medal, and the other Code Talkers were awarded the Congressional Silver Medal.

The role of the Navajo community in WWII was invaluable. Once almost extinct, the language went from being unknown beyond the borders of the Navajo reserve to one of the world's most revered languages. It laid the foundations for a highly innovative and complex military code that contributed to the Allies' success and baffled Japanese cryptographers for several years. Unlike any of its kind, this code was interpreted in only a few seconds and transmitted without error. The success and adversities faced by the Native Americans, especially the Navajo community, are a testament to their lasting resilience, determination, and impact of World War II.

Chapter 5: Vasily Zaitsev: The Eastern Sniper

Vasily Zaitsev is a name some Americans and others in the West might have heard of thanks to the movie "Enemy at the Gates." Although the movie is riddled with inaccuracies, it familiarized many with this Russian hero.

Vasily is one of the most famous snipers in the world.

Vasily is one of the most famous snipers in the world. He had an influential role during WWII that cemented his name in history. He killed about 300 Nazi soldiers and played a massive role in many battles contributing to the Soviet victory.

This chapter covers the life of Vasily Zaitsev and the battle that earned him a place in history.

The Early Life and Upbringing of Vasily Zaitsev

Born into a simple family in March 1915, Vasily had an interesting upbringing that prepared him for the role that changed his life and the course of history. He grew up in Yelenovsk, a village in the Chelyabinsk Region in the Urals, isolated from society. They didn't have grocery stores or outlets to buy food, so they had to become self-sufficient.

His grandfather, Andrei Alekseevich Zaitsev, taught him and his siblings hunting from a very young age. Unlike children their age who spent time playing and enjoying their child-like innocence, Vasily, his brothers, and cousins spent their days tracking wolves, setting traps, and sleeping outdoors, even during the cold. When he turned 12, he hunted his first wolf. Vasily was surprisingly talented as he managed to kill the wolf with one bullet, which was quite an accomplishment for a boy his age. He learned to hunt deer and rabbits and soon excelled at it and became the pride of his family.

Bullets were hard to come by, so hunters had to be careful not to waste them. For this reason, Vasily was taught to use only one bullet when hunting, which shaped his sharpshooting skills.

Even though he was still a child, Vasily had his personal weapon, a single-barreled rifle. It was so big he struggled to carry it on his back since he had an unusually small frame. It is believed that his grandfather gifted it to him. He used his weapon to sharpen his shooting skills, making him the killing machine that put fear in the hearts of thousands of Nazis.

Vasily had a rugged upbringing, which significantly impacted his personality and shaped him into the tough and strong soldier he was. Thanks to his grandfather, he learned the necessary skills to become one of the best snipers in history. He admitted that he owed his success as a sniper to his upbringing. He learned patience from stalking his prey and hiding for hours, becoming invisible until he could get the perfect shot. Vasily was a strong boy with remarkable self-control for someone so young.

Education

Vasily's hunting trips didn't distract him from his schoolwork - he was a clever, driven, and exceptional student. He graduated from seven classes in high school. In 1930, he graduated from the construction college in the city of Magnitogorsk. After graduation, he also studied accounting.

Vasily's Military Career

Vasily was destined to become a soldier from a young age. He had all the qualities to be a great sniper, such as military cunning, endurance, composure, sensitive hearing, and visual acuity.

In 1937, he worked as a clerk in the Soviet fleet's finance department in Vladivostok, Russia. However, he was a hunter and a soldier at heart, and an office job filing papers didn't fulfill him. He wanted to be out there chasing, hunting, and using the skills his grandfather had taught him.

In 1937, he joined the Red Army. Even though he had a small frame for a young man his age, he was recruited into the Soviet Navy. But this still wasn't enough for the Soviet hero, who had a lot more to offer. In September 1942, the Germans invaded the Soviet Union, so he and some of his fellow soldiers volunteered to join the frontlines. However, his request was denied four times. Fortunately, the fifth time was the charm, and he was assigned to the 1047th Rifle Regiment of the 284th Rifle Division of the 62nd Army, who fought in the Stalingrad battle.

When Vasily was transferred to the frontlines, he was a Sergeant Major. It was obvious to all from the start that he wasn't an ordinary soldier. He was exceptionally brave. Even when wounded multiple times, he never left his post; his country and the war came first. He was driven by his patriotism and courage.

Soon, Vasily became one of the most prominent soldiers. He got the attention of his superiors, especially during his first encounters with the Nazis. They could see his true talents and that his place wasn't on the frontlines.

One day, his superior officer asked to see him. He wanted to test his other skills. He showed him a soldier on the enemy lines and told him to shoot him through the window. It wasn't an easy shot, as the man was 2,500 feet away. Like he did with the wolves and deer years ago, Vasily killed the man with a single shot. When the German soldiers noticed he was down, they rushed to check on him. Vasily could see them from his window and killed each with one shot. This act earned him the Medal of Valor and a cash reward. It was at that moment that his true career and his heroic story as one of the world's best snipers began.

The Battle of Stalingrad

Vasily's killing streak wasn't slowing down. He had killed 32 Nazi soldiers with a simple sniper rifle. He was awarded a rifle with an optical sight, which he used to make history.

In September 1942, he arrived at Stalingrad across the Volga River. The soldiers had been fighting for a month, and the city had turned to rubble. However, the destruction allowed Vasily to easily hide and shoot his enemies.

Between November and December, Vasily shot and killed 225 German soldiers in the battle of Stalingrad. He made a name for himself in his home country and among his enemies. Among the men Vasily killed were 11 snipers, a substantial achievement that earned him the respect of his fellow soldiers and made the Germans tremble at the mention of his name. He became an inspiration to his troops, who were motivated by his skills to work harder and better themselves.

The Battle of Stalingrad lasted five months and ended with the Germans surrendering, giving the Soviets victory.

According to official records, Vasily killed 243 Germans. However, many believe the actual number is much higher, and many consider him a legend to this day.

Vasily War Tactics

Vasily used clever tactics to catch his enemies off-guard. He knew how to surprise them and where to hide from them, usually choosing the last place they would expect. He hid in different locations, like water pipes, under rubble, or on high ground. He would shoot a few men from one place and then change his location before he could be found.

Another common tactic he often used was covering a large area from different locations so he could kill more than one soldier at a time. This tactic was called the "Sixes," and many snipers worldwide still use it today. Another tactic Vasily used was going on daily and intense missions to neutralize marksmen, officers, and other military targets.

His tactics were influential and transformed sniper methods in the Soviet Union and worldwide. Modern sniper schools still teach his techniques and tactics.

It may seem that Vasily didn't have a hard time eliminating German soldiers. However, this isn't true. War is never easy. Some men were hard to find and harder to kill, like Heinz Thorvald, aka *Erwin König*.

Erwin König

The Germans became frustrated with Vasily, the legendary sniper who shot hundreds of their men, and no one could find him. So, they took action and sent one of their best men after him.

Vasily described Erwin König in his memoir as brilliant and a "Highly skilled sniper."
Bundesarchiv, Bild 169-0526 / CC-BY-SA 3.0, CC BY-SA 3.0 DE

Erwin König, or as Vasily described him in his memoirs, the "Supersniper," was the head of a sniper school in Germany and a high-ranking officer in the Nazi army. Little is known about Erwin, making him one of the most mysterious figures in the war. It is believed that he went to Stalingrad to destroy Soviet snipers and kill Vasily, who wreaked havoc on the German army and destroyed the soldiers' morale.

However, Vasily wasn't aware of Erwin's arrival, giving the German soldier a head start. It was only when a captured German officer boasted that Vasily's days were numbered because Germany sent their best sniper after him that he knew he was in danger. Soviet commander Nikolai Filippovich Batyuk assigned Vasily the mission of finding and killing Erwin.

Vasily was a confident man, so Erwin's skills didn't threaten him. He described him in his memoir as brilliant and a "Highly skilled sniper." Vasily mentioned that he spent a week looking for him, and the mission was challenging. However, when one Soviet sniper was shot and wounded, and another was shot and his optical sight broken, Vasily could determine Erwin's position.

He and another soldier, Nikolai Kulikov (Vasily's trusted friend, who fought side by side with him), tricked Erwin into revealing himself. They put a helmet over a stick to make it look like a soldier hiding, hoping Erwin would shoot at it and they would know his location. Their plan worked. After Erwin shot at the helmet, he lifted his head to see whether his target was alive or not. Vasily saw him and shot him, immediately killing him. This famous duel was featured in the movie "The Enemy Gates."

There are many speculations about this duel, and some people believe it never happened – and there was no German soldier named Erwin König. After much research, historians couldn't find strong evidence to prove these events occurred. All their information about the duel came from Vasily's memoirs or Soviet military records.

Vasily mentioned him by two names, Erwin König, and Heinz Thorvald. It is believed that these could have been the names of any two German soldiers with no relation to the man described in Vasily's book. Neither was there mention of an Erwin König in any German documents. If this man was a high-ranking officer, as Vasily and the Soviets claimed, finding records of him would have been easy. They claimed that Erwin killed 400 soldiers when the highest kill by a German sniper was 345 and belonged to Matthäus Hetzenauer.

The Soviets also exaggerated Erwin's achievements, making him seem like a superhuman rather than an ordinary soldier. Moreover, there was no sniper school in Germany, and the Germans didn't send a soldier named Erwin to Stalingrad.

So, did Erwin König exist? Maybe. During the war, many countries resort to rumors and fake stories to create a tough image of themselves to scare their enemy. This story was believed to be either heavily modified, contained inaccurate information, or didn't happen at all! Moscow's Armed Forces Museum claims they have Erwin's telescopic sight – however, there is no way to prove whether it was his.

On the other hand, military historian Antony Beevor extensively researched Erwin and the duel and found that they were all Soviet propaganda.

Whether this part of Vasily's story happened or not shouldn't matter since the man was a legend with or without this duel, and nothing and no one could belittle his achievements.

Temporary Blindness

In 1943, Vasily and a group of 13 snipers were sent to disrupt a German attack. However, there was a colossal mine explosion that left him wounded and blind. A plane was sent to his location immediately, taking him to a hospital in Moscow. Luckily for the Soviet army, the blindness was only temporary, and after several operations, he regained his eyesight and returned to battle.

Stalingrad Sniper School

In the first few days of the battle, Vasily killed about 40 German soldiers. His commanders were so impressed with his achievements they asked him to train new snipers. They established a sniper school in Stalingrad, the location of one of the bloodiest battles in WWII. Vasily taught in the school until his injury in 1943.

The school was vocal about the psychological toll of the war on Soviet soldiers. Vasily knew firsthand what the war could do to a person's mental health, and he often spoke about it in interviews. He wanted his school to play a role in reducing the impact of the war on the Soviet soldiers.

The school awarded the best student with Vasily's rifle. His students killed about 6000 men during the war.

Vasily's Legacy

In November 1942, the Soviets were struggling and about to lose Stalingrad, a city they held dear. They were desperate and hopeless until something happened that raised their morale and made them believe they could win. Vasily's arrival changed the course of the battle and gave the Soviets an advantage.

At the beginning of the battle, no one was aware of Vasily's unique skills. During a German counterattack at Stalingrad, many Russian soldiers lost their lives. Vasily and a few of his comrades survived. However, they were stuck behind the German lines. Fortunately, he found a rifle, killed the guards, and escaped with his men.

Reports of his heroic act reached his superiors, who finally recognized his talents. It was also published in Moscow's newspaper. When the Russians read about Vasily's bravery, they were filled with hope and believed their soldiers could win the war.

Vasily became a symbol of hope and resistance. The Russian people believed that if one man was capable of these heroic acts, then the entire army was also capable of great things.

After the war, Vasily spent his days in Kyiv. He studied at the Institute of Textile and Light Industry. His war days were behind him as he became a garment factory director in Ukraine and headed a light industry technical school. On December 15, 1991, Vasily passed away, leaving behind a significant legacy and a memory of a great soldier who was willing to die for his country.

When talking about soldiers, people usually focus on their skills or the number of people they killed and forget the human behind these stories, the one who witnessed the horrors of the war.

Vasily was a vicious warrior who killed his enemies without hesitation. However, like any soldier, this war left its toll on him. He spoke about the impact of the Stalingrad Battle and the images of dead children that haunted him and left this great warrior shaking.

Vasily became one of the most famous heroes in Russia's history for his bravery and tactics to win the battle.

Although the war made him one of the most famous soldiers in the country, Vasily didn't care about fame or the glory it brought him. He was a clever man who had his priorities straight. He knew nothing should come before his country, so he focused on his mission.

When you think of Vasily, don't remember him as the man who killed over 200 German soldiers or the fearful figure that frightened them. Vasily was more than that. He symbolized Soviet resistance, resilience, and indomitable spirit during one of the deadliest battles in history. The outcome would have been very different if he hadn't joined the battle.

Vasily was born to be a sniper. This man was destined to spend his life stalking prey, from everything he learned as a child to his love for hunting and adventure. He became a Russian hero thanks to his skills, war tactics, and devotion to his country. Vasily was a beacon of light during the war's darkest hours, making people believe they could get through these tough times. He was the man whose name terrified the Nazis.

Even though he had a rough childhood, faced hardships in life, and was wounded multiple times, he never let anything affect his spirit or love for his country.

Chapter 6: Audie Murphy: America's Most Decorated

Audie Murphy was the most decorated soldier of WWII. His life story is an inspiring vision of disregarding your safety for the benefit of others. Many of Murphy's valiant actions were him leading from the front so the people under his command could be spared. From his childhood, earning money and hunting to care for his siblings to his rise as a soldier, Murphy always lived his life selflessly.

Audie Murphy was the most decorated soldier of WWII.
https://commons.wikimedia.org/wiki/File:Audie_Murphy_uniform_medals.jpg

He was described as small with a sickly greyish complexion, probably resulting from his poor upbringing and malnutrition. At a glance, you would never guess that this hero could move swiftly and fearlessly through the battlefield. The skilled marksman navigated the frontlines with unmatched courage. The 5'5" "giant" stood tall as a hero among heroes, achieving unparalleled greatness on and off the battlefield.

Murphy's advocacy for mental health paved the way for a deeper understanding of PTSD. The brave man was unafraid to show his vulnerabilities to benefit other veterans who needed help. In a time when the mental health of soldiers was ignored or taboo to discuss, Murphy broke the mold and alerted the public to the lasting impacts of war. His countless medals and tireless work for veterans made Audie Murphy one of the greatest warriors to have walked the planet. Audie Murphy's life symbolizes that no matter what people think about you or your physical and mental limitations, you can achieve anything if you are inspired by something more significant than yourself. His allergy to quitting and hard work put him miles ahead of many who were served a better start in life than he.

Childhood, Enlistment, and Rejection

Murphy's destiny to become one of the most important figures in WWII and a Hollywood superstar could not have been predicted based on his humble beginnings. He was born on a sharecropping farm in Texas in 1924 to parents, Emmett and Josie Bell Murphy, who were of Irish descent. The young boy understood hard work from an early age as the Texan sun beat down on the back of his neck while he picked cotton for a dollar per day. Murphy never completed school and was orphaned at 16. Growing up, he did not have much, but his parents did the best that they could. From a young age, Murphy had to contribute to the household, teaching him a profound sense of responsibility.

Furthermore, Murphy grew into suffering, enabling him to thrive in the horrific and excruciatingly difficult environments of the war. He was the sixth child of 12 children, nine of whom survived until adulthood. He would later be reunited with his three younger siblings after the war, taking them under his wing. Murphy's military skill was only matched by his big heart that he hid under a tough exterior.

Murphy was a master with a rifle hunting small game, like most farm boys of his era. His hunting prowess often put food on the table, so his family encouraged his skill. In addition to working on a sharecropping plantation, Murphy worked at a general store and filling station in Greenville, Texas. Murphy's father had abandoned the family, and his mother tragically passed in 1941. The 16-year-old was forced by circumstance to look for employment, resulting in him working diligently at a radio repair shop. His mother's death was devasting for the teen because it split his family, with three of his younger siblings forced to live in an orphanage. The others went to live with relatives willing to take them in.

Through the suffering of his early life, Murphy may not have recognized it, but his remarkable character was strengthened in the furnace of adversity. Murphy had become accustomed to difficulty, so no adjustment period was needed to embrace the extremities of war. His life was an uphill battle from a young age, so he had to fight for survival. His gigantic, resilient spirit dwarfed Murphy's small physical stature. Not many people could go through what Murphy experienced and emerge more determined and focused. Some people break under pressure. Murphy thrived in it.

The challenges of life weighed heavy on the talented young man's shoulders. The only escape he envisaged was to join the military. Murphy was on the shorter side, standing at 5'5", and his impoverished background never allowed him to gain height, so he had a scrawny frame of only 110 pounds. His height and weight resulted in him getting rejected from joining the Marines and the paratroopers. At 17, he finally joined the U.S. Army by falsifying his documents, stating he was a year older. After the grueling basic training at Camp Wolters in Texas, the eager young serviceman completed advanced training at Fort Meade. He was assigned to the 15th Regiment, 3rd Infantry Division in North Africa after completing advanced training.

Murphy was heavily underestimated, and many wondered if he would be a capable soldier. His company commander wanted him to train to be a cook and a baker, but Murphy insisted he wanted to see active combat. He believed in his abilities and felt better suited for the front lines. Time would prove Murphy right as he became the war's most decorated soldier. His hardened bravery could not be replicated because he was bred from a life of difficulty. In Africa, Murphy never saw any action, but his time there contributed to his overall growth as a soldier. His extensive training maneuvers with his regiment prepared him for the intense fights he would encounter.

Remarkable Acts of Valor

In his first combat experience, Murphy proved that his company commander made the right decision by allowing him to enter the fight. In 1943, during the invasion to liberate Sicily, Murphy displayed the marksmen abilities he had been honing hunting small game since his childhood. Murphy fought in the Voltuno River campaign and was part of the Allied Forces that would make their way into Rome. He quickly rose through the ranks as officers got injured or were transferred to other areas. His skills were finally recognized as he proved himself battle-ready.

The first decoration Murphy received was the Medal of Honor, the highest decoration a person can receive in the U.S. Military. The award dates back to the American Civil War and has had various iterations until the 1904 Gillespie version Murphy received. In January 1945, the Germans attempted to take back the strategically valuable wooded region of Bois de Riedwihr near Holzwihr in France. The intimidating Germans menacingly marched forth to the woods with infantrymen and six state-of-the-art tanks.

After an officer had been wounded, Murphy took command of the B. Company. Murphy only had 18 men on his side to face the terrifying German force quickly approaching. He had two M10 tanks, far inferior to the German's armor, at their disposal and indirect artillery fire for support. In a selfless act of heroism, Murphy commanded his men to retreat while he stayed to direct the artillery fire using a telephone. The Germans directly hit one tank, putting it out of commission early in the battle. Murphy stood atop the tank, firing at the Germans between calling to direct the artillery. Once the telephone broke, all that was left was one man and his machine gun. The Germans did not know which direction the bullets were coming from, so it was hard to pin him down. After sustaining too many casualties, the Germans retreated. A lone soldier was able to stop the well-equipped infantry with their tanks, earning Murphy the Medal of Honor.

The following decoration that Murphy earned was the Distinguished Service Cross, an award of valor just underneath the Medal of Honor. In August 1944, the 1st Battalion, 15th Infantry Regiment, and the 3rd Infantry Division commenced a first wave of attack in the South of France. Murphy's platoon advanced on a hill where the enemy combatants were stationed. Murphy, concerned about the safety of his men, ordered them to stay behind while he advanced to determine if the enemy was obstructing their path. Armed with an M-1 Carbine, Murphy went forward to uncover the enemy positions. He fired, killing two enemy soldiers before retreating down the hill because he ran out of ammunition. He grabbed a machine gun from one of his crew, who was scared stiff, unable to proceed up the hill. He gunned down more German foxholes, destroying their positions.

Once he depleted the machine gun ammo, he went back down the hill to grab his carbine again. This time, his close comrade Lattie Tipton convinced Murphy to let him assist. They came under heavy fire from machine gunners, and Tipton was tragically killed in the fight. He died by the bullet of a coward who waved a fake flag of surrender to draw the deceived Tipton nearer. Before Murphy got a chance to stop his friend, it was too late. In a fit of uncontrollable rage, Murphy utterly destroyed the remaining gunners with righteous indignation. Murphy carried the deceased Tipton down the hill, consumed with despair.

The next award Murphy received was the Silver Star with Oak Leaf Cluster. In October 1944, Lieutenant Colonel Michael Paulick, Lieutenant Colonel Keith L. Ware, Captain Paul Harris, and four more soldiers went to the frontlines of Cleurie Quarry to identify where German machine gunners were hidden because they hindered the battalion's ability to move forward. The machine gun fire resulted in several casualties. Murphy was unhappy with this plan and warned them that the hidden snipers and gunners would cause problems. As they left, Murphy secretly trailed behind them at about 25 yards.

As Murphy expected, machine gunners opened fire on the group. He yelled their names to let them know he was planning to save them, and they could take cover. The machine gunner turned to Murphy, but his gun got caught on a shrub, causing him to miss. Murphy took advantage of the mistake and threw a couple of grenades before firing and killing two Germans. He killed another two and wounded three. Another soldier attempted to flee, but Murphy spotted and killed him.

Three days later, Murphy earned another Silver Star. He led his 72-man platoon over a hill in the North of Cleurie along a dry creek bed. German soldiers hid along the creek and, spotting the platoon, opened fire with machine guns and sniper rifles. The Germans killed seven men. The other platoons that were part of the company stayed hidden and waited for Murphy to provide information. Murphy's platoon proceeded forward, attempting to stay covered, but nobody knew where the bullets were coming from. Eventually, Murphy commanded his men to stay covered while he moved forward alone. He spotted the machine gunners and snipers opening fire on them. He used his walkie-talkie to call indirect fire onto their exposed positions. Any Germans attempting to take cover were quickly eliminated. 15 Germans were killed, and 35 were wounded. Murphy, once again, displayed the power of individual action.

After receiving his two Silver Stars, Murphy received another military decoration, a Legion of Merit. The medal was awarded for his exceptional performance in the field in Italy and France. This award was more for his broader achievements than a specific battle. He received the decoration because he fearlessly completed his missions with elite abilities regardless of the danger. The award was given to him by General Alexander M. Patch in Austria on June 2, 1945. He received the Medal of Honor and the Legion of Merit on the same day. Murphy had an endless list of further decorations, including a Bronze Star, a Purple Heart, an Outstanding Civilian Service Medal, a Good Conduct Medal, and an Army of Occupation Medal, all totaling over 30.

Mental and Physical Struggles

Even though he had a tough upbringing, the horrors of war still scarred Murphy tremendously. Unlike many other soldiers who attempted to maintain a facade of toughness, Murphy openly spoke about his mental issues. Murphy suffered from PTSD, which is still common in soldiers returning from active combat today. All the decorations Murphy received could not save him from the lingering tortures of combat, even after the war had ended. He described how he had no internal peace, felt irritated in crowds, and constantly conflicted about whether he needed company or wanted to be alone. It was almost like he was a walking ghost who had to pretend to be human. Murphy was lost in society after being profoundly changed by the war.

In WWII, PTSD was known as "battle fatigue," and in the First World War, it was called "shell shock." Both names denote the same phenomenon because no living person is meant to endure the death and destruction directly involved during a war. As psychological and scientific research advances, more is understood about PTSD. Unfortunately, in the years following WWII, little was known about the condition, and nobody knew how to treat it. Murphy had to grin and bear the mental torment until his death.

Even today, PTSD is a common problem many people suffer from. In America, about 7% of the population is suffering from the disorder, many of whom are veterans who turn to substance abuse (Smith, 2015). Greater awareness is needed for the disorder because many do not get the help they deserve - many veterans end up homeless on the street because, in large part, of untreated PTSD. Therefore, the government has to put in much more effort to ensure the well-being of the service people – often forgotten after putting their lives on the line to serve their country.

Murphy's PTSD manifested in many physical symptoms like insomnia and vomiting. Nightmares of war constantly tormented him. His PTSD caused him to become addicted to sleeping pills. After successfully kicking the habit, he realized that he was not the only soldier experiencing PTSD and addiction. Murphy abhorred that the government would just give their soldiers a pension and send them on their way without doing anything to address their adversely impacted mental state. He became an outspoken advocate for providing veterans with proper care. Murphy's activism was revolutionary at the time because it was impolite to speak about the war in peacetime, and many saw it as an invasion of privacy to ask soldiers about their combat experiences. His selfless heroism extended beyond the battlefield as he worked hard to create a better life for his brothers in arms.

The detail Murphy went into when describing his struggles enlightened much of the public on the harsh realities of war. He spoke about how war destroys mentally and physically. He couldn't feel excited for anything, and he remained in constant paranoia. Murphy slept with a gun by his side and even pulled it on his wife once, causing their divorce in 1951.

Memoir and Hollywood

After his time in the war, Murphy became a successful actor who starred in over forty feature films. His handsome and boyish good looks made him the perfect leading man. However, he is still mainly remembered as the most decorated soldier of WWII. Hollywood screenwriter and veteran David McClure encouraged Murphy to write a memoir of his experiences during his active combat. Murphy took his advice and obtained a book deal with Henry Holt and Co. with McClure as his ghostwriter.

The book's name was <u>To Hell and Back</u>. But writing it was frustrating and tedious. Murphy, as an introvert with PTSD, struggled to speak about the finer details of his experiences, which annoyed McClure, who wanted to write the best book possible. Murphy wrote about 10% of the book, and McClure finished the rest by relying on medal citations to obtain the facts. He also used the popular book by Donald Taggart called "History of the Third Infantry Division in World War II."

Murphy and McClure would revisit some places where intense battles occurred that were essential to Murphy's story. Getting Murphy to speak in detail was like pulling teeth without anesthetic. However, he sometimes went into the finer aspects of his life story, adding authenticity to the book. Murphy rejected the first few attempts of the book, which often upset McClure, who was doing his best in a challenging situation.

The book does not take long to dive into action, beginning with his introduction to combat in Sicily. It captures the intense violence, fear, and uncertainty that occurred in the heat of battle. The 300-page book, an easy read, was later made into a film in 1955, where Murphy played himself as the leading role. The book is not highlighted as one of the best works of WWII, but the film is considered a classic. Audie Murphy did not believe his acting skills were the greatest, but he stuck with the career path because he could not survive solely on a military pension.

At 46, Murphy died in a plane crash. He was buried in Section 46, across from the Memorial Amphitheater. Due to the vast number of people paying their respects to Murphy, a flagstone walkway was constructed.

Chapter 7: Raoul Wallenberg: The Swedish Savior

This chapter aims to navigate the complexities of Nazi-occupied Hungary, centering on Raoul Wallenberg's humanitarian mission to save its persecuted Jewish population. After introducing Wallenberg, a Swedish diplomat with no connection to Hungary, underlining the international scope of his endeavors, the chapter outlines his innovative use of "protective passports."

Wallenberg played a vital role in establishing safe houses under Swedish protection, which became sanctuaries for thousands of Jews.
https://commons.wikimedia.org/wiki/File:Raoul_Wallenberg_214082a.jpg

Additionally, you'll learn about Wallenberg's role in establishing safe houses under Swedish protection, which became sanctuaries for thousands of Jews. Highlighting Wallenberg's daring confrontations with German and Hungarian officials, including when he valiantly intervened in deportations and death marches, this chapter also details the strategic alliances he formed with other diplomats and underground movements to amplify his rescue efforts. Lastly, you'll learn about Wallenberg's mysterious disappearance in January 1945 after being detained by Soviet authorities.

The Early Years

Born into two distinguished families in 1912 in Stockholm, Raoul Wallenberg was a son of Maj Wising, a daughter of a prominent neurologist, and his father, also named Raoul Wallenberg, a celebrated naval officer. However, his father died before he was born, and his mother remarried soon after. While close to his mother, stepfather, and step-siblings, Raoul lived with his paternal grandparents during his early years. His grandfather, Gustav Wallenberg, the Japanese Ambassador of the Swedish embassy, took care of young Raoul's education. Wanting to liberate his grandson from the narrow worldviews of the early 20th-century Swedish wealthy society, Gustav set on making him a citizen of the world. However, he hoped that Raoul would embark on a journey to continue the family tradition and become a politician or a banker when he finished his early education and explorations across the globe. Upon completing secondary school and the compulsory military training in Sweden, Raoul was sent to France for a year to become fluent in French (he already spoke German, Russian, and English). Then, Gustav sent Raoul to the United States to study architecture, wanting his grandson to absorb American culture's practicality (since he had no intention of entering banking or politics).

After graduating in 1935 with honors, Raoul returned to Sweden, intending to work as an architect. His plans were spoiled when he learned that his US degree wasn't recognized in Sweden, so he traveled to South Africa, where he worked for six months. He transferred to a bank in Palestine, working for a Jewish banker from the Netherlands, who was Gustav's friend (the elder Wallenberg was still hoping his grandson would join the family business). It was here that Raoul was first faced with growing anti-Semitism. Through his Dutch mentor, he met numerous Jewish refugees who flew to Palestine from Germany and other countries. He was astounded to learn that some of these refugees once belonged to wealthy families, and after the Nazi regime stripped them of their rights, they lost their standing and weren't even considered people anymore.

Diplomatic Efforts

When Gustav Wallenberg died in 1937, Raoul lost his sponsor, mentor, and confidant. He tried to start two businesses for the next four years, with no success. Meanwhile, he couldn't forget about the Jews' ordeal in Germany and tried to help refugees in Sweden. Finally, in 1941, through Jacob Wallenberg, his uncle and godfather, he obtained employment at the Central European Trading Company. The business was owned by Kalman Lauer, a Hungarian Jew, who saw an immense opportunity in employing Raoul at his export-import enterprise. After all, young Wallenberg could travel freely across Europe and was fluent in several languages, whereas Lauer encountered numerous difficulties when trying to sell products in Central Europe. It wasn't long before Wallenberg became the firm's international manager and Lauer's business partner. His business trips took Wallenberg to several European countries, including France, Germany (both occupied by the Nazis), and Hungary. While conducting business in Germany, Wallenberg learned the ins and outs of German bureaucracy - information he would find rather useful in the future. In Hungary, he found a country he grew to love, so he was moved by the events that followed.

The Germans Invade Hungary

After the Nazis occupied Hungary on March 19, 1944, the Hungarian government handed over 450,000 Jews living in the country. Adolf Eichmann, the officer sent to oversee the deportation of Jews in Hungary, worked diligently in sending them over to the Nazi death camps. While he began collecting Jews in the countryside, he slowly worked his way to the capital, Budapest, where the wealthy Jewish families resided in a strong community. Determined to wipe all Hungarian Jews off the face of the earth, Eichmann targeted the families living in Budapest. In a belated attempt to stop Eichmann, the American government sent their American War Refugee Board representative, Iver Olsen, to Stockholm. After an improvised negotiation between the World Jewish Congress, the Swedish Foreign Ministry, and the American War Refugee Board, it was decided that Sweden would send a diplomat to oversee the rescue of Jewish families in the Hungarian capital. They just had to find the right man for the job.

Olsen was tasked to look for someone who could travel to Hungary, spoke German and Hungarian, and was willing to put their lives at risk by violating the German military law and going against Hitler's grandiose plans to complete the project he called "Final Solution." After a chance encounter with Kalman Lauer, Olsen learned that Raoul Wallenberg might be the man he was looking for. He made an offer to Wallenberg, who jumped at the opportunity to make a difference.

The Heroic Work in Hungary Begins

On July 9, 1944, Raoul Wallenberg arrived in Hungary as a diplomat of the Swedish embassy in Budapest. However, while other Swedish officials were subject to heavy restrictions, he insisted on having more freedom, which he certainly needed given the work he was about to undertake. By this time, the Swedish and other neutral legislations were issuing provisional passports across Europe. But the Jews also needed other means of assistance, especially in Hungary. Olsen tasked Wallenberg to help accelerate the process of providing these measures. After the insistence of King Gustav V of Sweden, the Germans stopped using deportation trains in Hungary, but they kept transporting the Jews to labor camps at the Austrian border via other means. A few weeks before Wallenberg arrived in Hungary, Valdemar Langlet, a Swedish Red Cross worker, became part of the protective network established by the Swedish legation. Renting buildings on behalf of the Red Cross and disguising them as research institutes, libraries, and other public facilities, Langlet set up safe spaces for Jews fleeing from the Nazi deportation attempts.

Wallenberg's first step after arriving in Budapest was to establish an office and hire 400 people to work for him. They were all Jews, and they were ordered to remove the traditional yellow stars they wore (as this could easily identify them as Jews). They were now under Swedish diplomatic protection but still in danger from the Nazis. This step was only the first part of the remarkable work Wallenberg did over the next six months in an attempt to save the remaining Jews in Hungary.

Next, Wallenberg printed the Schutzpass, a special Swedish passport that ultimately saved the lives of tens of thousands of Jews in Budapest. Knowing the German bureaucracy's weakness for symbolism,

Wallenberg designed the passport as a colorful, official-looking document with lots of blue and yellow, the traditional Swedish colors. He added the Swedish coat of arms in the front center and the appropriate signatures and stamps. Despite his lack of background in diplomacy and authority to grant immunity to anyone (and having just created a false document), Wallenberg persuaded the Hungarian Foreign Ministry to approve the print of 4,500 Schutzpasses. He had already printed a thousand copies himself and then printed three times more than what was approved. He distributed the passports to the Jews, stating it would grant the holder immunity from deportation.

Funded by the American government, Wallenberg rented 32 houses in Budapest and placed them under the protection of Swedish diplomatic immunity. This was the continued effort toward his relief work, as these properties were converted into safe havens for the endangered Hungarian Jews. The refugees found shelter and protection under neutral legislation in these so-called "Swedish houses" (which belonged to the same relief network Valdemar Langlet used). They were given passports, directions, guidance, and funds to travel to another neutral territory if they wanted to.

In the following months, tens of thousands of Jews found solace in the houses rented by Wallenberg. His architectural training in the United States contributed significantly to the success of this effort. Knowing how to design a building that could fit many people into a confined area, Wallenberg had no problem placing 35,000 refugees in a building only meant to hold a seventh of that. As more and more people sought refuge and passports, Wallenberg streamlined the printing process and designed a simplified version of the document. The new passport only had his signature. By this time, everyone in the Jewish and Hungarian diplomatic community knew Wallenberg's name. The conditions in the country were chaotic, so he could easily pass this false passport as an official document.

A renowned professor at the University of Michigan, Andrew Nagy, was saved through Raoul Wallenberg's efforts. Nagy, staying at a safe house with his mother, witnessed the residents from his neighboring home being taken from their beds and executed at the bank of the Danube River on Christmas Eve 1944. According to other witness reports, the Nazis had a peculiar practice of tying three people together and shooting only the middle person on the Danube's shore. As the dead person fell into the river, the other two went with them into the freezing water and subsequently froze or drowned. When Wallenberg heard of this practice, he recruited a few good swimmers among his sizable volunteer staff and took them to the Danube. They jumped into the freezing river water and looked for survivors. Using this extraordinary method on several occasions, they rescued 50-60 people, freeing them from their ties and removing them from the water.

All these efforts left Wallenberg with no more than 3-4 hours of sleep a night. He didn't mind because his conscience wouldn't let him sleep soundly, knowing that people were being executed and not doing everything he could to prevent it. Over time, he became an inspiration to the Swedish diplomats and everyone else on a humanitarian mission in the Nazi-occupied countries across Europe. Swiss neutrals and Red Cross workers remarked on his boldness, while those who actively worked on Wallenberg's side found him the most courageous man they had ever known. However, the ones to whom his work meant the most were those who lost hope and believed they were doomed, witnessing their community members fall. Thanks to Raoul Wallenberg, they found hope and trusted that they'd survive the cruel destiny imposed on them by the Nazis.

Wallenberg's Life Is Threatened

Since Wallenberg couldn't hide his activity from the Nazis, he resorted to unusual methods to ensure the German officials wouldn't hinder his objectives. These included bribing, harassing, confronting, and manipulating German and Hungarian officers to overlook his attempts to rescue the Jews. These methods induced heavy skepticism in other neutral diplomats, but when they realized how effective they were, all doubts about Wallenberg doing the right thing were dissipated.

Adolf Eichmann, who learned about his methods, named him "Jewdog Wallenberg," expressing his disdain for the Swedish savior's work. By the winter, Wallenberg became aware of the pending danger over his life and frequently switched residences. There were several attempts to kill him, including when his vehicle was bombed.

After learning about the Soviet troops' imminent arrival and threat over the German forces, the latter accelerated their efforts of liquidating the Hungarian Jews. In mid-November 1944, Eichmann ordered thousands of Jews to be led away from Hungary on foot. Supported by the Hungarian Nazis, the German officers gathered in the largest Jewish community, preparing to shoot everyone. Once again, Wallenberg stepped in, convincing the German commander in charge to call off the pending massacre. By this time, Hitler was about to be defeated, so when Wallenberg told the Nazis that the attack would lead to them receiving the death penalty for crimes against humanity after the war ended, they believed him. It's estimated that by preventing the atrocious assault, Wallenberg saved 70,000 lives that day. He provided them with shelter, medicine, food, and passports.

At the beginning of the following year, the Soviet forces reached Hungary. Moreover, while the Germans fled Hungary, the local Nazis remained and were scouring the streets of Budapest, looking for Jews to kill. This lasted for two months (numerous lives were lost at the hands of the fanatic Hungarian Nazis) until the Soviet troops occupied the city. In the meantime, Raoul Wallenberg learned to speak Russian, hoping to establish an alliance with the Soviet leaders and gain their assistance in rehabilitating the city's demolished society.

Disappearance and Possible Death

On the morning of January 17, 1945, a large group of Soviet officers knocked on Wallenberg's door. Using his primitive Russian, Wallenberg explained the scope of his work and asked the officers to lead him to their superiors so he could explain more. He was led to the Soviet headquarters in Budapest, where he spent the night, after which he was ordered to return home, pick up his belongings, and let the Soviets escort him away. He calmly picked up his possessions, reassuring his colleagues that he would get the help they needed and would be back in a week. He was never seen alive again. According to some sources, Wallenberg placed the reconstruction plan (after working on it extensively during the last two months) into his briefcase, taking it with him on this last journey. To this day, no one knows why he was detained instead of being allowed to outline his plan. Some claim the Soviets may have believed that he was an American spy. Others assume his connection with German and Hungarian politicians (which he only used for relief work) was the motive for his arrest.

It's unclear what happened to him after his detainment. By April 1945, Swedish authorities learned about Wallenberg's disappearance and investigated. After being asked about his whereabouts, the Soviet authorities claimed that Wallenberg was not held by them. However, Swedish prisoners released from the Soviet Union in the early 1950s claimed they'd seen Wallenberg in a Moscow prison. With renewed efforts to find their countryman, the Swedish pressured the Soviets for an answer. In 1957, the Soviet authorities claimed that Raoul Wallenberg was arrested and died in prison in July of the same year but never explained the reasons for his detention. While some claim that he lived for much longer in prison, the Soviet authorities issued a report (based on a prison document dated July 17, 1947) indicating that the Swedish diplomat died from a cardiac infarction after a few months of imprisonment. This raised even more suspicion because an infarction was often used to conceal the actual reason behind a prisoner's death. The authenticity of this investigation is still disputed.

After over 30 years of negotiations between Russians and Swedish diplomatic forces, in October 1989, there was a breakthrough in Raoul Wallenberg's disappearance case. His family was asked to travel to Moscow, where they were handed his passport and other belongings. After many years of joint investigation by the Soviet and Swedish governments, another report about Raoul Wallenberg's fate was issued. While it didn't clear up key questions, like the reason for his imprisonment, the Soviets admitted that Wallenberg didn't die of natural causes. No further proof was found as to what truly happened to him and when. With so many unanswered questions, the Swedish government refused to close Wallenberg's case file. In 2016, the Swedish Tax Agency officially declared Wallenberg dead, putting his date of death to July 31, 1952, five years after his disappearance.

Raoul Wallenberg's Enduring Legacy

Despite uncertainties surrounding his fate, Raoul Wallenberg's legacy still lives on. His valorous deeds are celebrated worldwide as a beacon of hope and courage amid the darkest chapters of human history. By the end of World War II, his protective passports are rumored to have saved over 20,000 lives. The survivors and their descendants will never forget his name. They will forever remember him as a young man with an outstanding decisiveness to act in the name of humanity. Beyond sheltering Jewish refugees, Wallenberg conducted tireless negotiations and contributed to various neutral diplomatic missions, including the International and Swedish Red Cross rescue efforts and the Papal Nunciature.

Wallenberg acquired outstanding international acclaim, including an honorary citizen of the United States in 1981. He received the same title from Canada, Israel, and Australia in 1985, 1986, and 2013, respectively. In the decades after his disappearance, numerous monuments and works of art were named after him, and his name became cemented into history through books, movies, musical pieces, and other sources honoring and detailing his achievements, which speak about the importance of fighting against racism. Raoul Wallenberg's legacy serves as a reminder that every individual has a responsibility to take a stand against discriminatory and violent acts against other races, and their actions can make a difference.

Chapter 8: Nancy Wake: Gestapo's Most Wanted

Spies played an influential role during World War II. In France, they supported the Allies against the German occupation. One was Nancy Wake, whose story resembles a James Bond movie with high-risk operations, intelligence gathering, specialist training, and dedicated technology.

Nancy was the perfect spy thanks to her courage and adventurous spirit.

Nancy was the perfect spy thanks to her courage and adventurous spirit. She served honorably, and her role in the Second World War made her a heroine. Her exciting story was featured in the 2014 movie, "Nancy Wake, the White Mouse."

This chapter covers the thrilling escapades of this indomitable woman who had the whole of Germany after her.

Nancy's Upbringing

Born on August 30, 1912, in Roseneath, Wellington, New Zealand, Nancy Grace Augusta Wake was one of the key figures in the French Resistance. She was the daughter of journalist Charles Augustus Wake and Ella Rosieur. It was clear that Nancy would lead an interesting life from the moment she was born. After her birth, the midwife told Ella that her newborn would be a very lucky girl and the gods would always protect her. Ella always reminded her daughter of this story, but Nancy never felt fortunate.

Nancy and her family moved to Sydney when she was about two years old. She spent her childhood there and attended the North Sydney Household Arts School. Sadly, she didn't have a happy childhood, and many events prepared her for her future role.

Nancy loved and admired her father, and they shared a strong bond. However, when she was four, he went to the U.S. for work but never returned. It was heartbreaking for the little girl who was very close to her father. This incident taught Nancy to think twice before trusting anyone again.

Her mother, Ella, was a cruel and heartless woman. She never gave her daughter any affection and often told her she didn't love her. Although Nancy lived with her mother, she never felt she had parents. She became independent from a very young age and cleaned, cooked, and earned her own money, enforcing in her that she could handle anything on her own.

Another event that shaped Nancy's personality occurred when she had to tell on her best friend, Jenny, to save herself. The look of betrayal in Jenny's eyes changed Nancy forever. At this moment, she decided never to cross a friend again.

Nancy hadn't been close to her siblings since they were much older, and she never felt they had anything in common. When she turned 16, she ran away from home and worked as a nurse under a false name for two years. When she turned 18, she returned to Sydney, where she worked on a farm and kept her distance from her family.

At the age of 20, Nancy's aunt died, leaving her a small inheritance. She took the money and traveled to Europe to begin the journey of a lifetime that changed her life and influenced the events of World War II.

Nancy's Life in France

Nancy first traveled to the U.S. before traveling to London in 1932, where she studied journalism. Her thriving new career took her to Paris a year later. She worked as a journalist at the Hearst newspaper chain. She reported on the rise of the Nazi movement, which left her sick and angry at the injustice the Jewish people faced. Nancy's job took her to many places around the world, like Vienna, where she witnessed the Nazi violence firsthand. She was consumed with hatred toward these people and vowed that if she ever had the opportunity, she would do everything in her power to end their reign of terror.

In 1936, Nancy fell in love and married French millionaire Henri Fiocca. She quit her job as a journalist and enjoyed the lavish lifestyle. However, her happy life didn't last long, and soon, Nancy would leave everything behind for the sake of the greater good.

In 1940, Germany invaded France, and everything that appalled Nancy was now close to home. It was the opportunity she had been waiting for to stop the Nazis. She and her husband joined the French Resistance, and Nancy became their courier – the beginning of her life as a spy. She carried messages and advanced radio parts from the French Resistance to secret partisans.

Since she was the wife of one of the wealthiest men in the country, no one suspected she would join the resistance and become a spy. Wives of wealthy men were seen as spoiled women without a care in the world. This stereotype, albeit unfair, was an excellent cover for Nancy and helped her avoid getting caught. So, when someone suspected her or she was in a tough situation, she resorted to her beauty and cunning personality. She flirted with the German guards to pass checkpoints. She mentioned in an interview that being a woman gave her an advantage. It was easy for a woman to get out of trouble with a wink and a little powder.

The resistance was very impressed with Nancy's work and depended on her in multiple missions. She used her privileged position and asked her husband to buy her an ambulance, which she used to transfer Jewish refugees, Allied pilots, and Dunkirk survivors to safe houses until they could arrange to move them to Spain. Nancy created false identities and documents to aid her in her life as a spy.

Soon, she became the resistance's top spy. As a result, she got the attention of the German police, also known as the Gestapo. She used her different identities and intelligence to evade them. They got close to catching her a few times, but she always managed to escape. Once, the Gestapo had her surrounded and shot at her, but she got away. They taped her phone and watched her every move, but she was always one step ahead of them. Her elusiveness earned her the nickname "The White Mouse."

Nancy became the Gestapo's number one most wanted with a price on her head of five million francs. Life became very dangerous for Nancy, so the resistance thought it safer for her to go to Britain. However, the journey was perilous.

Nancy's Dramatic Escape

Nancy left her husband behind to escape to Britain. She planned to cross the Pyrenees Mountains but faced many challenges. She was arrested in France and spent four days in prison. A friend made up a story that helped get her released. She was arrested again in Spain, but she managed to escape again. Nancy's journey to Britain was like something out of an action movie. German soldiers were shooting at her, she spent days without food and water, she hid in sheep pens, she slept in the streets in the cold weather, almost suffering from hypothermia, and she jumped from moving trains to run from German soldiers. After six attempts, Nancy finally arrived in England. But something tragic happened that she didn't learn about until after the war.

The German police arrested her husband, Henri, hoping he would give them information about her. They tortured him, forcing him to tell them her whereabouts, but Henri loved his wife and refused to say a word. When they realized he wouldn't speak, they executed him.

Nancy's Life in England

After arriving in England, Nancy was ready to fight Hitler and the Nazis. She joined the Special Operations Executive or SOE using the alias First Aid Nursing Yeomanry or FANY. The SOE was a prominent organization established by Winston Churchill to assist resistance movements throughout Europe.

The SOE had heard about Nancy's work in France and was impressed by her courage, loyalty, and determination. When they heard about her arrival in England, they didn't hesitate and recruited her immediately. Her colleagues in the SOE raved about her. They described her as an "Australian bombshell" with a strong fighting spirit, cheerful attitude, and infectious energy. Her training reports were exceptional. She was a fast shot, had unmatched craft skills, and was stronger than most of the men in the training program.

Her training made Nancy an expert in hand-to-hand combat, explosives, prospering behind enemy lines, and guerrilla warfare. She was one of 39 women in the SOE's French section. Their leader was Colonel Maurice Buckmaster, who was involved with different resistance groups to destroy German forces in France, Poland, and other countries.

The SOE gave Nancy her first assignment as a saboteur. The mission involved many sleepless nights, coordinating, planning, motivating, and training the Maquis to prepare for D-day. The Maquis were a French resistance group who performed guerrilla warfare and helped Allied officers.

However, one aspect of the task kept her up at night - parachuting safely from an airplane to land in her second home, France.

In 1943, Nancy and a group of 39 women and 430 men parachuted into the forests of L'Auvergne in France. Nancy got tangled in a tree and was saved by the Maquis leader, Captain Henri Tardivat. Henri couldn't resist Nancy's beauty and flirted with her. However, she didn't have the time for silly conversations and expressed her disinterest in a firm tone.

Interestingly, Henry and Nancy became close friends, and he named his daughter after her. He admired her femininity and strength.

Nancy acted as a liaison officer between the Maquis and England. Upon her arrival, she discussed the resistance situation in France with Henri and his men. She was surprised there wasn't any method of communication with the English. They were stranded and had no way to reach out to the SOE. But Nancy had her D-Day plans and a large amount of money, so she was confident she could complete the task. Nancy's mission was to allocate equipment and arms and judge the strength of radio frequencies.

Nancy used the alias "Madame Andrée" when interacting with the partisans. However, they didn't respect her as they believed she was just a beautiful woman who used her sexuality to get what she wanted. Nancy decided to teach them a lesson. She engaged their leaders in drinking contests and beat them all. The men realized she wasn't an ordinary woman and viewed her differently from then on.

Nancy quickly proved her value to the Maquis. She recruited over 7,000 men, making them one of Europe's most powerful resistance groups. She also led multiple attacks against German installations.

Before D-Day, Nancy succeeded in restoring communication with the resistance in Britain. She took that opportunity to organize parachute drops with England. In a short time, she gathered the explosives and weapons for her mission. She trained the new recruits and taught them discipline. She didn't want soldiers who were only good with weapons. She wanted them to be brave and quick and to think on their feet. So, she did everything in her power to foster these qualities in them.

Nancy and the Maquis were ready for D-Day.

On June 6, 1944, also known as D-Day, the Maquis began their attacks, but Nancy was missing as she went to pick up a weapon's instructor. They blew up several German targets, hoping to weaken their forces. When Nancy returned, she felt bad for missing all the fun. But their mission wasn't over yet. Nancy and her men wrecked trains, blew up bridges, and ambushed the Germans.

Nancy proved to be a courageous warrior. The partisans described her as braver than all their men.

Four days later, the Germans retaliated and launched severe attacks on the Maquis. Denis Rake, the man responsible for wireless communication with England, was afraid of getting caught, so he burned his codes and hid his equipment. Nancy couldn't communicate with the SOE, so she had no choice but to look for another operator.

500 KM Bike Ride

Nancy rode about 500 km on her bike to Chateauroux to find a new operator. It was a long and arduous journey that many of her superiors thought she couldn't make. They believed it was beyond her physical capabilities since she was a woman. They whispered among each other, "How could a woman travel a long distance through harsh roads?" Others believed she was insane for taking this trip as she would be defenseless and exposed, especially as the Gestapo's most wanted. However, Nancy knew she could make it and return unharmed with the new operator.

She began her journey at night and often rested on roadside barns. Although extremely tired, she was determined and only focused on her goal rather than how she felt. She encountered a few German soldiers on her journey but used her charm and flirted so they wouldn't search her. In less than two days, she found an operator, and they agreed to parachute a new wireless set to the desired location. She completed her mission, got on her bike, and returned to her camps.

This may sound like an easy trip, or you might think it was just another day in the life of a brave soldier and spy. However, when Nancy returned, she was in excruciating pain. She couldn't sit, stand, or move. When others asked her how she felt, she merely cried. This humanizes Nancy. Even though she was a fearless soldier who could kill a man with her bare hands, she was still a human who felt pain and cried when she couldn't handle it.

Although Nancy had accomplished many things during the Second World War, she often said she was most proud of this mission and rode her bike for about 500 KM in three days. Interestingly, she never rode a bicycle again for the rest of her life.

Killing German Soldiers

Many stories highlight Nancy's personality and what she was willing to do for the cause. Although some showed her as a cold-blooded murderer, the reality was different.

She once found her men were protecting a female German spy as they struggled with killing a young girl. Nancy killed her without hesitation. She later said that she didn't regret her actions because war required making harsh decisions.

She once said the only good German soldiers were the dead ones, and she wanted many of them killed to prevent their injustice and cruelty toward the Jews.

She killed a German sentry agent by slitting his throat to prevent him from alerting the guards to her presence. Although this might seem cold-blooded, this wasn't who Nancy truly was. She mentioned in multiple interviews that she hated killing people but refused to sit at home and watch the men fight when she knew she could make a difference. Desperate times called for desperate measures, and she had no other option.

Nancy's Famous Nickname

German soldiers gave Nancy a very unusual nickname, "The White Mouse," because of her ability to get away and escape even though there was a huge price on her head. Nancy was the Nazis' worst nightmare, but she was Winston Churchill's golden girl and one of his most decorated agents. You wouldn't have guessed that she was a soldier by looking at her. Nancy was always well-kept with red lipstick, and her hair was coiffured. You would assume she was heading to a party, not fighting a war. However, this was part of her cover. Who would guess this glamorous woman was Gestapo's most wanted?

However, once she came face to face with her enemies, she was fierce and deadly, with or without her weapon.

Legacy

After the war, Nancy rushed home to look for her beloved husband, only to find that he had chosen death over betraying her. When she received the terrible news, her heart broke. Henri was the love of her life, and for the rest of her life, she blamed herself for his death. In 1957, she married John Forward, but they didn't have children. She led a quiet life until she died in 2011 at the age of 98.

She wrote her autobiography, titled "The White Mouse," after her famous nickname, which became a New York bestseller. Nancy tried to get into politics a few times but failed, so she and her husband retired to Australia. John died in 1997. In 2001, she moved to England, where she spent the rest of her days. She celebrated her 90th birthday in a hotel in London. The owner refused to let her pay and took care of all the expenses.

Nancy was awarded multiple medals in her lifetime, including:
- The George Medal
- The Medal of Freedom

- The Chevalier de la Légion d'Honneur
- The Croix de Guerre
- The Medaille de la Resistance from France

Nancy was awarded multiple medals in her lifetime.

She remained one of the most respected figures in history for her bravery and her role in destroying the Nazis' powers in Europe. However, Nancy didn't receive any awards from Australia since she didn't serve her country. A few years before her death, the Australian government contacted her because they wanted to award her with a medal. She refused to accept it. She believed it was too late for that gesture. It wasn't offered to her out of admiration or love. They were pressured to do it or to save face. Either way, Nancy felt that their sentiments weren't genuine. However, in 2004, they made her a Companion of the Order of Australia, and later, she received the RSA Badge in Gold, New Zealand's highest honor.

The little girl whose beloved father abandoned her and a mother who never loved her didn't let the adversity bring her down. Even though her parents betrayed her, Nancy eventually learned to love and trust again. She became a heroine who sympathized with the weak and those who didn't have a voice. She spoke for them in the only language the enemy understood, the language of violence. She was a fierce warrior respected by everyone who met her. Years after her death, she is still remembered as a war heroine and female idol who showed the world that women could do much more during the war than stay home waiting for their husbands to return.

Chapter 9: The Tuskegee Airmen: Skies of Change

World War II was a pivotal era in global history, marked not only by the ferocity of battle but also by the prevailing social and racial attitudes of the time. As the United States actively engaged in the conflict, a shadow of segregation hung over its military forces, with racial barriers deeply rooted in the fabric of the armed services. During this tumultuous time, a group of African-American military aviators emerged as heroes, challenging the deeply rooted racial prejudices. This is the story of the Tuskegee Airmen, a squadron of black pilots who defied skepticism, prejudice, and adversity to become war heroes and pioneers in the fight for civil rights.

This is the story of the Tuskegee Airmen, a squadron of black pilots who defied skepticism, prejudice, and adversity to become war heroes and pioneers in the fight for civil rights.

To understand the significance of the Tuskegee Airmen's journey, first, you must understand the backdrop of racial segregation that plagued the United States during World War II. African Americans faced a paradoxical situation as the country mobilized for war in the early 1940s. While they were expected to contribute to the war effort, they did so in an environment rife with racial discrimination. The U.S. military, like much of the nation, adhered to a policy of segregation, relegating African-American soldiers to inferior roles and limiting their opportunities for advancement.

This discriminatory backdrop set the stage for the skepticism the Tuskegee Airmen would confront. Despite the prevailing belief that African Americans were unfit for combat roles, a visionary initiative was born – the Tuskegee Airmen program. Established at the Tuskegee Institute in Alabama, the program aimed to train black pilots for combat, challenging the deeply ingrained notion of racial inferiority.

The training program was no ordinary undertaking. Under the leadership of Captain Benjamin O. Davis Jr., the first African American to graduate from West Point, and Chief Civilian Flight Instructor Charles Alfred Anderson, the Tuskegee Airmen underwent rigorous training that mirrored the challenges they would face in the theater of war. The Tuskegee Airmen's training included flight instruction and intensive physical and mental conditioning, preparing them for the demanding realities of aerial combat.

As the Tuskegee Airmen honed their skills, the world outside their training grounds was embroiled in the chaos of war. The early 1940s saw the Axis powers, led by Nazi Germany, expanding their control across Europe and North Africa. Against this backdrop, the Tuskegee Airmen were deployed to North Africa and later to the European theater. Their distinguished combat record quickly dispelled any doubts about their capabilities.

One of the notable achievements of the Tuskegee Airmen was their reputation for protecting bomber crews. In the perilous skies over Europe, they flew escort missions for American bombers, facing off against formidable German fighter planes. Their success in these missions earned them the respect of bomber crews, highlighting their skill, courage, and the effectiveness of their training.

The Tuskegee Airmen were not merely combatants in a war. They were architects of change. Their exemplary service during World War II became a catalyst for the eventual desegregation of the U.S. armed forces.

Tuskegee Institute Training

Against the backdrop of a racially segregated America in the early 1940s, a transformative initiative took flight. Driven by the vision of Tuskegee Institute's President, Dr. Frederick D. Patterson, and buoyed by the advocacy of First Lady Eleanor Roosevelt, the Tuskegee Airmen program emerged in 1941. This groundbreaking endeavor sought to defy racial stereotypes by training African American pilots and challenging the discriminatory norms that restricted their roles in the war effort.

The inaugural class, known as Class 42C, comprised 12 cadets and a single student officer, Capt. Benjamin O. Davis Jr. His pivotal role later unfolded within the 332nd Fighter Group. In March 1942, Class 42C earned their wings at the Tuskegee Army Airfield, marking a historic moment as the nation's first black military pilot. However, despite this achievement, deployment orders were conspicuously absent. Following extended delays by the War Department, the 99th Fighter Squadron, a 400-strong unit, finally deployed to North Africa in April 1943. Over time, the 99th merged into the larger 332nd Fighter Group, which included the 100th, 301st, and 302nd African American Fighter Squadrons stationed in Italy.

Tuskegee Institute, a historically significant African-American educational institution, became the epicenter of a pioneering experiment in military integration. However, the training regimen was no cakewalk. It was a demanding crucible intended to equip these aviators with flying skills and the resilience and mental acuity required for the challenges of military aviation.

The physical demands of the Tuskegee Airmen's training were no joke either. Their training included pre-dawn runs, obstacle courses straight out of a boot camp movie, and weightlifting sessions that pushed these men to their limits. The purpose was to ensure these pilots were in peak physical condition to endure the strains of combat.

At the center of this physical conditioning was Chief Civilian Flight Instructor Charles Alfred Anderson, affectionately known as "Chief." His famed obstacle course became a symbol of the grit required for aerial combat. The hurdles, climbing walls, and simulated combat scenarios weren't for show. They were a testament to the physical prowess these aviators needed.

Flying a plane in wartime isn't only about technical know-how. It's about split-second decision-making under immense pressure. The Tuskegee training program simulated combat situations that tested the mettle of these aviators. Captain Benjamin O. Davis Jr., a trailblazer in his own right, instilled a culture of discipline and determination. His leadership wasn't about settling. It was about reaching for excellence, a standard he expected his men to meet.

The Tuskegee Airmen's training created skilled pilots as a deliberate effort to shatter racial stereotypes. The program aimed to produce exceptional aviators and prove that African Americans could excel in complex and demanding roles within the military.

The instructors at Tuskegee, including Charles Alfred Anderson and Major Noel Parrish, were educators, mentors, and symbols of achievement. Major Parrish, who became the chief flight instructor, brought a wealth of experience, ensuring that the training wasn't theoretical but grounded in the practicalities of wartime aviation.

As the Airmen progressed through their training, they became proficient in flying and a closely-knit unit. The challenges they faced together, whether in the obstacle course or simulated combat scenarios, forged a camaraderie that would prove indispensable when they faced the real challenges of combat.

The Tuskegee Institute training program was more than a preparation for war. It was a crucible of transformation. It not only equipped these individuals with the skills for aerial combat but also played a pivotal role in reshaping perceptions about the capabilities of African Americans in the military. The resilience, determination, and brotherhood forged at Tuskegee were the unsung heroes behind the Tuskegee Airmen's success and their enduring impact on American history.

Deployment and Combat Record

When the Tuskegee Airmen, the trailblazing all-black military pilot group, took to the skies, they weren't only challenging gravity - they defied the gravity of racial prejudices. Deployed to North Africa and later Europe during World War II, their journey was a saga of overcoming the enemy planes and the skepticism and discrimination that dogged them from the start.

In North Africa, the Tuskegee Airmen, officially known as the 332nd Fighter Group, had their first taste of combat. Operating from bases in Tunisia and later Italy, they flew P-40 Warhawks and the renowned P-51 Mustangs. Their missions ranged from escorting bombers to engaging enemy aircraft, showcasing their versatility and adaptability.

One of the Tuskegee Airmen's standout achievements was their reputation for being bomber protectors. In the perilous skies over Europe, escorting bombers was no small feat. The B-17 Flying Fortress and B-24 Liberator bombers were the lifelines of strategic bombing campaigns but were vulnerable to enemy fighters. The Tuskegee Airmen, with their distinctive red-tailed planes, became synonymous with bomber protection.

Their prowess in safeguarding bombers earned them the nickname "Red Tails" from the bomber crews they escorted. The red markings on their planes served as a marker of identity and a symbol of reassurance for the bomber crews. The Tuskegee Airmen's success in this crucial role not only defied the doubts about their abilities but also highlighted their exceptional skill in combat.

The Tuskegee Airmen weren't flying for show. They made history. One of their most celebrated missions was the escort of bombers to Berlin on March 24, 1945.

The escort mission to Berlin stands out as a defining moment in the Tuskegee Airmen's history. This mission culminated their training, skills, and determination and marked a significant stride in their fight against the enemy in the air and racial prejudice on the ground.

The decision to assign the Tuskegee Airmen the crucial task of escorting bombers to Berlin was not arbitrary. It was a testament to their commanders' trust and confidence in their abilities. Berlin, the heart of Nazi Germany, represented a formidable challenge in distance and the intensity of enemy defenses. The mission was a strategic move aimed at striking the heart of the Axis power and proving the Tuskegee Airmen's mettle in one of the most challenging scenarios of the war.

The distance covered during this mission was substantial, involving a round trip of hundreds of miles. The journey took the pilots deep into enemy territory, where they had to navigate the complex and dangerous airspace controlled by the German Luftwaffe. The risks were numerous – from enemy fighters to anti-aircraft fire. The Tuskegee Airmen had to confront the physical challenges of flying for extended periods and the psychological strain of being in the heart of enemy-controlled skies.

Despite these challenges, the Tuskegee Airmen delivered on their mission with exceptional effectiveness. The bomber crews they escorted were a lifeline for the Allied war effort. The Tuskegee Airmen's role was to fly alongside the bombers and provide a shield, a protective barrier against the deadly German fighters eager to intercept them.

The Tuskegee Airmen showcased their combat effectiveness in the face of fierce opposition. They engaged enemy aircraft, fending off attacks and ensuring the safe passage of the bombers. The success of this mission was a military achievement and a powerful statement about the capabilities of African-American pilots in a theater of war dominated by racial biases.

The successful escort mission to Berlin had a ripple effect beyond its immediate military impact. It became a symbol of African-American excellence and valor, challenging the deeply ingrained stereotypes about the ability of black soldiers. The Tuskegee Airmen demonstrated their aerial combat proficiency and capacity to contribute significantly to critical strategic operations.

This historic mission contributed to a shift in perception within the military and the broader American public. The Tuskegee Airmen fulfilled a duty and broke barriers. The red-tailed planes that flew over Berlin symbolized Allied airpower and the determination to overcome prejudice and discrimination.

Another milestone where their name shines brightly is Lieutenant Lee Archer, a member of the Tuskegee Airmen whose groundbreaking achievement altered the course of history. In a defining moment during World War II, Archer became the first African American pilot to shoot down a jet-powered aircraft – a German Me 262.

At the time, the Me 262 was a technological marvel, the world's first operational jet-powered fighter aircraft. Its speed and maneuverability posed a significant threat to Allied forces. The existence of this advanced German aircraft pushed the Allies to adapt and enhance their strategies constantly. Facing such cutting-edge technology, the achievement of shooting down a Me 262 was not only a personal victory for Archer but also a testament to the Tuskegee Airmen's capabilities as a whole.

The encounter with the Me 262 occurred on October 12, 1944, during a bomber escort mission near Linz, Austria. Archer and his fellow pilots were flying P-51 Mustangs, their iconic red tails marking them as Tuskegee Airmen. The Me 262, boasting incredible speed, was a formidable adversary. Archer's engagement with this advanced German jet was a personal confrontation, a clash of technologies, and a symbolic battle against racial prejudice.

Archer's successful takedown of the Me 262 shattered deeply ingrained racial stereotypes that questioned the black pilots' capabilities. The prevailing belief was that African-American pilots lacked the skill and competence for high-stakes aerial combat, especially against advanced enemy aircraft. Archer's achievement defied these stereotypes and became a powerful rebuttal to the discriminatory practices within the military and society at large.

The Tuskegee Airmen faced skepticism from the enemy and from within their own ranks. Some doubted their ability to carry out complex missions effectively. However, their combat record spoke louder than any prejudice.

Their success in protecting bombers silenced skeptics, earning them the respect and admiration of the bomber crews they supported. The crews soon realized that having the "Red Tails" as escorts meant a higher likelihood of making it home. The Tuskegee Airmen changed the course of the war and the minds of prejudiced people.

Lieutenant Colonel Benjamin O. Davis Jr., who led the Tuskegee Airmen as they transitioned to P-51 Mustangs, was pivotal in bridging the gap between the bomber crews and his pilots. His leadership was crucial in fostering camaraderie between the Tuskegee Airmen and the crews they protected. This respect wasn't only about military efficiency. It was about breaking down racial barriers within the armed forces.

The Tuskegee Airmen's deployment in North Africa and Europe was a military campaign and a transformative chapter in the ongoing battle against racial discrimination. Their dedication, skill, and courage in the face of adversity contributed to the Allied victory and left an indelible mark on the history of civil rights in the United States. The red tails that streaked across the skies symbolized protection: a symbol of progress, breaking through the clouds of prejudice that lingered over the nation.

Post-War Impact

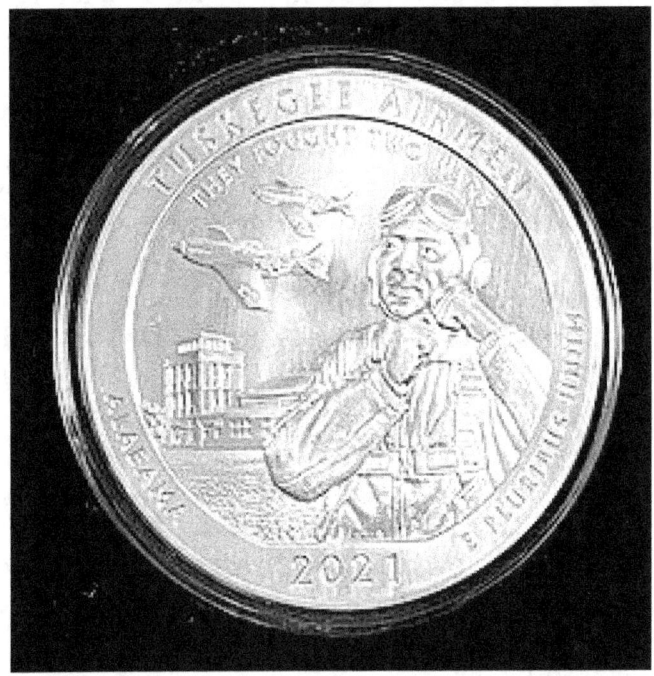

The Tuskegee Airmen's legacy fueled the civil rights movement, pushing for equality in a society stuck in discrimination.

The Tuskegee Airmen weren't only heroes in the war; they became trailblazers for civil rights when the fighting was over. Black pilots soared through the skies, proving they were every bit as skilled as their white counterparts. Their daring feats in World War II shattered myths that black folks couldn't handle the pressure. They flew planes and challenged racial stereotypes.

Think about a young African American child in the 1940s, seeing heroes who looked like them. The Tuskegee Airmen were living proof that color had nothing to do with courage and competence. Their legacy fueled the civil rights movement, pushing for equality in a society stuck in discrimination.

Fast forward to 1948, President Truman finally said, "Enough is enough." He signed an order ending racial segregation in the military. The Tuskegee Airmen, with their red-tailed planes, had punched a hole through prejudice.

After the war, the Tuskegee Airmen didn't hang up their flight suits. Their courage and skill had cracked the foundation of segregation. The military couldn't ignore that these guys, who happened to have darker skin, had proven themselves as real American heroes.

By 1948, segregation was officially kicked out of the military. It was a victory for both the Tuskegee Airmen and common sense. The red tails had helped bring about a change that rippled through the armed forces, showing that excellence had nothing to do with a person's skin color.

Lee Archer, after breaking records by shooting down a German jet, didn't stop. Archer became a leader in aviation, proving that the sky was no limit for a man of his caliber. Benjamin O. Davis Jr. rose to become the first African-American general in the U.S. Air Force. These men weren't just flying high. They were breaking through racial barriers, opening doors for others to follow.

Together, the Tuskegee Airmen didn't merely fade into the background. They became advocates for change. They spoke out against discrimination and became role models for a new generation. Their shared experiences formed a bond that went beyond the cockpit. They were a force of change, pushing for justice and a fair share for everyone, no matter their background.

Imagine being a child in the 1950s, dreaming of flying like those red-tailed heroes. Besides flying planes, the Tuskegee Airmen inspired a whole generation. They went into schools, encouraging black youth to reach for the skies, showing that dreams could soar higher than prejudice.

Those red tails were symbols of progress. Their success in the war paved the way for more opportunities for African Americans. It was more than about flying. It was about proving that everyone deserved a fair shot, regardless of their skin color.

Their story didn't fade away. Books, documentaries, and movies, like "Red Tails," brought their achievements to the forefront. Their legacy became part of American culture, ensuring their courage and determination were celebrated and remembered.

Ultimately, the Tuskegee Airmen's story isn't just another war tale. It's a story of heroes who flew through the clouds and broke through the barriers of prejudice. Their legacy doesn't just exist in the past. It's a living reminder that bravery, skill, and determination can change the course of history and pave the way for a more equal and just future.

Chapter 10: Chiune Sugihara: The Japanese Schindler

In the chaotic landscape of World War II, a remarkable figure, Chiune Sugihara, took center stage. Serving as the vice-consul in Kaunas, Lithuania, in 1940, Sugihara was in a world overshadowed by the looming horror of the Holocaust. As Europe grappled with the tightening grip of the Nazi regime, Sugihara's journey unfolded as a beacon of hope amid the prevailing darkness.

As Europe grappled with the tightening grip of the Nazi regime, Sugihara's journey unfolded as a beacon of hope amid the prevailing darkness.

Powerful nations were fighting for control, and the Nazis, led by Hitler, were spreading their influence across Europe. This period marked the horrifying Holocaust, where the Nazis aimed to wipe out entire communities, especially targeting Jewish people.

Kaunas, the capital of Lithuania, became a significant battleground in this global struggle. The city faced the uncertainties of changing alliances and the occupation of territories. The situation was dire, especially for Jewish refugees trying to escape persecution. Borders were tightly controlled, and fear hung in the air like a thick fog.

Imagine Sugihara's role in this intense environment. His decisions were crucial as he dealt with the Jewish refugees' desperate pleas. The geopolitical complexities added layers of difficulty, and escaping seemed almost impossible. Sugihara's choices in Kaunas would become a lifeline for those fleeing persecution.

This chapter details Sugihara's story and explores the challenges and dilemmas he faced during this critical period. Against the backdrop of global upheaval, Sugihara's actions are a testament to the resilience of the human spirit. As you read, you will discover a man whose decisions defied orders, reshaped destinies, and ultimately earned him the moniker of the Japanese Schindler.

Sugihara's Role as Vice-Consul in Kaunas

Chiune Sugihara assumed the role of vice-consul in Kaunas, Lithuania, in 1940, a position that thrust him into the heart of a maelstrom of historical events. Born on January 1, 1900, in Yaotsu, Japan, Sugihara's early life provided a foundation for the values that would later define him. Growing up in a family of modest means, Sugihara was instilled with a strong work ethic and a deep sense of responsibility.

His academic prowess led him to study at Waseda University, where he delved into languages and pursued a degree in English. His proficiency in languages would prove instrumental in his diplomatic career. Sugihara's early exposure to different cultures and languages laid the groundwork for the cosmopolitan outlook that would distinguish him in later years.

After completing his studies, Sugihara entered the Ministry of Foreign Affairs in 1934, embarking on a diplomatic career that would take him to various postings, including Manchuria and Helsinki. These diverse assignments cultivated Sugihara's adaptability and diplomatic acumen, preparing him for the challenges he would face in Kaunas.

The vice-consul's duties represented Japan's interests in Lithuania, a country caught in the crossfire of changing allegiances and the ruthless advance of the Nazi regime. Sugihara's diplomatic position became critical due to the geopolitical complexities unfolding during World War II. Lithuania, facing the brutal occupation of the Nazis, saw a dramatic shift in its political landscape, and Sugihara had to navigate the challenges of a nation in turmoil.

As Sugihara began his tenure in Kaunas, the Holocaust was in full swing across Europe. Hitler's sinister plan to annihilate entire communities, mainly targeting Jewish people, had reached a horrifying crescendo. The Nuremberg Laws, stripping Jews of their rights, and the ghettos established by the Nazis marked the early stages of a tragedy that would reverberate through history.

Lithuania, with its substantial Jewish population, became a focal point of Nazi atrocities. The infamous Einsatzgruppen, the mobile killing squads, descended upon the country, committing mass shootings and spreading terror. Jewish communities faced unspeakable horrors, and the urgency to escape became a matter of life and death.

Sugihara's office in Kaunas became a sanctuary for those desperately seeking a lifeline. Jewish refugees, aware of Japan's more lenient visa requirements, flocked to the consulate, hoping for salvation. The initial encounters between Sugihara and these desperate individuals were characterized by profound desperation and fear.

Facing a tidal wave of pleas for transit visas, Sugihara was caught between the rigid regulations of his superiors in Tokyo and the harrowing stories of those standing before him. The refugees, often holding heartbreaking documentation of persecution, were seeking passage through Japanese-controlled territories to escape the Nazis' clutches.

Sugihara, torn between duty and compassion, grappled with a moral dilemma that would define his legacy. His decision to go against official orders and issue visas to thousands of Jewish refugees demonstrated an act of defiance and a profound commitment to humanity in unparalleled adversity.

One notable example is the "Sugihara Visa," which granted a reprieve to Polish Jews who had escaped to Lithuania. Despite facing intense pressure from his superiors and the diplomatic risks involved, Sugihara continued to issue visas, creating a flicker of hope for those on the brink of despair.

These courageous decisions marked Sugihara's journey as vice-consul in Kaunas, setting the stage for a humanitarian effort that would reverberate through history. As you learn more about the intricate details of this story, Sugihara's courage and compassion will illuminate humanity's path in one of its darkest periods.

Moral Dilemma and Strict Regulations

Chiune Sugihara's internal struggle during his time in Kaunas is a testament to the moral complexity of the horrors that the Holocaust unfolded. Imagine a man torn between duty and compassion, a diplomat grappling with the weight of human suffering that stood before him. Sugihara's internal conflict was not merely a clash of professional obligations but a battle waged in the depths of his conscience.

As he witnessed the desperation of Jewish refugees clamoring for visas, Sugihara's empathy collided with the strict guidelines set by his superiors. He was well aware that deviating from these orders could jeopardize his career, reputation, and his family's well-being in Japan. Yet, the faces of those seeking refuge haunted him, and the moral imperative to act weighed heavily on his shoulders.

One poignant account illustrates the depth of Sugihara's internal turmoil. Facing a queue of desperate refugees outside the consulate, he reportedly said, "Please forgive me. I may not follow the Ministry's directive. Forgive me. I will issue visas to all the refugees I can, even if I am fired."

This heartfelt expression encapsulates the profound struggle within Sugihara—a man standing at the crossroads of human suffering and bureaucratic rigidity, torn between the constraints of official orders and the call for compassion.

His predicament was exacerbated by the stringent directives emanating from Tokyo. His superiors, ensconced in the political realities of wartime Japan, adhered to a policy prioritizing diplomatic relationships over humanitarian concerns. The official stance was clear. Visas were only granted to those with proper funds and a confirmed route out of the Soviet Union.

Sugihara's defiance of these orders meant challenging the established protocols of the Japanese Foreign Ministry and the prevailing ethos of wartime diplomacy. His superiors, undoubtedly aware of the consequences these actions could bring, demanded strict adherence to policy. This clash between the rigid dictates of bureaucracy and the compassionate instincts of an individual would define Sugihara's legacy.

In an unfolding humanitarian crisis, Sugihara grappled with profound ethical considerations. The plight of Jewish refugees escaping the atrocities of the Holocaust forced him to confront the limits of bureaucratic reasoning and the cost of adhering strictly to official mandates.

One striking example of Sugihara's ethical considerations was his decision to issue visas to refugees even as the consulate was closing. Faced with an imminent departure, he continued to handwrite visas while on the train platform, extending a lifeline to those desperately awaiting escape.

The ethical dilemma intensified as Sugihara realized that the visas he issued went beyond the prescribed criteria. He assisted those with confirmed funds, exit routes, and even those lacking these prerequisites. He knowingly violated the established rules but remained steadfast in his commitment to alleviating human suffering.

Sugihara's ethical considerations were not abstract. They were manifested in tangible actions that defied the bureaucratic machinery. His decision to prioritize humanity over protocol would echo through history, leaving an enduring example of the individual's capacity to resist injustice within institutional constraints.

Defying Orders and Handwriting Thousands of Visas

The turning point in Chiune Sugihara's story unfolded when he made the courageous decision to defy official orders and issue visas to Jewish refugees against the directives from Tokyo. Faced with the harrowing reality of desperate individuals seeking refuge from the Holocaust, Sugihara chose humanity over bureaucracy.

He expressed the gravity of his decision in his own words, stating, "I may have to disobey the government, but if I don't, I would be disobeying God." This powerful declaration encapsulates the moral imperative that guided his actions. Despite the risks to his career and personal life, Sugihara took a stand against injustice, laying the groundwork for an extraordinary act of compassion.

His commitment to saving lives materialized in the meticulous and labor-intensive process of handwriting thousands of visas. The bureaucratic system demanded adherence to strict regulations, but he embarked on a marathon effort to process requests that extended into the late hours of the night.

The visas were not just pieces of paper. They were lifelines, symbols of hope for those on the brink of despair. Sugihara's dedication to this task went beyond the call of duty. With each stroke of his pen, he defied the orders from Tokyo and etched a path to freedom for the refugees.

One account recounts Sugihara's tireless efforts on the train platform as he continued to issue visas even as he prepared to depart. In those final moments, with the train about to pull away, he handed out visas through the windows.

The act of defying orders came at a tremendous personal cost to Sugihara. The repercussions were not only immediate but also echoed through the following years. His decision to prioritize human lives over bureaucratic protocol resulted in his dismissal from the Foreign Ministry in 1947. Sugihara, the man who defied orders to save lives, had to face the consequences of his actions.

Despite the personal sacrifices, Sugihara's legacy is measured in the lives he saved. Estimates suggest the visas he issued provided an escape for around 6,000 Jewish refugees. Each visa represented a family, a story, and a future that would have been extinguished by the Holocaust.

The impact of Sugihara's defiance extended beyond the immediate moment. The handwritten visas symbolized resilience and a testament to an individual's power to make a difference in overwhelming adversity. The sacrifices he made were not only professional. They were a testament to the human cost of doing what was right amid global turmoil.

Sugihara's decision to issue visas and his dedication to personally handwrite each one transformed the narrative of his diplomatic career into a beacon of hope. The refugees who escaped through the corridor created by those visas could build new lives, carrying with them the indomitable spirit of a man who dared to challenge the status quo.

The Life-Saving Corridor

Chiune Sugihara's extraordinary efforts extended beyond the issuance of visas. They encompassed the creation of a life-saving corridor through the Soviet Union, providing an escape route for Jewish refugees. This corridor became a beacon of hope, a narrow path through which thousands could journey from the clutches of the Holocaust to the possibility of freedom.

Sugihara's actions were not limited to defying official orders and handwriting visas. He recognized the situation's urgency and collaborated with Jan Zwartendijk, the Dutch consul in Kaunas. Zwartendijk assisted by providing travel documents to Curacao, a Dutch colony in the Caribbean. Sugihara issued transit visas, allowing refugees to pass through the Soviet Union to Japan and beyond.

This collaboration effectively created a humanitarian corridor, a lifeline for those who sought to escape the horrors of the Nazi regime. The journey through the Soviet Union, fraught with challenges, offered a chance for survival to those persecuted and desperate.

However, the creation of the life-saving corridor was not without its hurdles. The refugees faced a hazardous journey through the vast expanse of the Soviet Union, navigating its diverse landscapes and overcoming logistical challenges. The political climate added further complexities, with the Soviet authorities scrutinizing those passing through their territories.

Additionally, Sugihara's efforts met extensive resistance from his government. When the Japanese consulate closed in September 1940, Sugihara continued his work from a hotel, tirelessly continuing to issue visas. However, the visas were no guarantee of safety. The refugees had to traverse a precarious route through the Soviet Union, exposed to the uncertainties of war-torn territories.

Sugihara's dedication to the cause transcended the bureaucratic obstacles. He defied official orders to issue visas and continued to support the refugees even after the consulate's closure. The challenges encountered on this perilous journey were met with resilience as the refugees clung to the hope of a better future beyond the reach of Nazi persecution.

The impact of the life-saving corridor orchestrated by Sugihara and Zwartendijk was profound and far-reaching. Around 6,000 Jewish refugees, armed with transit visas, embarked on a journey that led them away from the imminent danger in Europe.

For those who successfully navigated the corridor, the impact was life-altering. Families were preserved, and individuals could rebuild their lives in safer havens. The testimonies of those who escaped through this humanitarian effort speak of physical salvation and the preservation of hope and human dignity.

One account is of Solly Ganor, a Lithuanian Jew who, as a teenager, obtained a Sugihara visa. Ganor and his family made the arduous journey through the Soviet Union and eventually settled in Japan. His subsequent recollections emphasize the corridor's transformative effect on the lives of those who survived the specter of annihilation.

The impact rippled through generations as the descendants of those who escaped through Sugihara's corridor flourished in countries far from the reach of Nazi oppression. Their stories became a testament to the resilience of the human spirit and the enduring power of compassion in adversity.

Recognition as "Righteous Among the Nations"

Chiune Sugihara's heroic actions did not go unnoticed. Decades later, Israel formally acknowledged his extraordinary contributions by naming him "Righteous Among the Nations." This prestigious title is granted by the State of Israel to individuals who risked their lives to save Jews during the Holocaust.

Sugihara's recognition stems from his defiance of official orders, the issuance of thousands of life-saving visas, and the creation of a humanitarian corridor allowing Jewish refugees to escape the horrors of the Nazi regime. The Yad Vashem Holocaust Memorial in Israel officially recognized Sugihara's selfless acts in 1985, honoring him as a hero who stood against the prevailing darkness of war.

Being designated as "Righteous Among the Nations" holds profound significance for the individuals recognized and the collective memory of the Holocaust. This title is a mark of honor and distinction, signifying an individual's unwavering commitment to humanitarian values, often at great personal risk.

For Sugihara, the acknowledgment of being "Righteous Among the Nations" posthumously affirmed the righteousness of his actions. It elevated his legacy beyond the confines of diplomatic history and positioned him among a select group of individuals recognized for their exceptional courage during one of humanity's darkest periods.

This recognition is a powerful reminder that heroism can emerge from unexpected places. Sugihara, a Japanese diplomat stationed in Lithuania, became an unlikely savior for thousands of Jewish lives, challenging preconceived notions of who could make a difference during the Holocaust.

Sugihara's legacy extends far beyond the recognition bestowed upon him. He symbolizes humanity's potential for good, even in overpowering evil. His story resonates as a beacon of hope, illustrating the impact one individual can have on the course of history when guided by compassion and moral conviction.

The recognition as "Righteous Among the Nations" solidifies Sugihara's place in the collective consciousness of those who reflect on the Holocaust. His legacy is an enduring testament to the power of individual agency in systemic injustice. Sugihara's story challenges people to consider their life choices and the profound impact that acts of kindness and moral courage can have on the world.

Moreover, Sugihara's contributions encourage a broader understanding of heroism. It reminds you that heroes come in diverse forms and from unexpected places. His legacy challenges the notion that heroism is the exclusive domain of the powerful or those in traditional positions of authority. Sugihara's story invites you to recognize and celebrate the potential for good that resides in every individual, emphasizing that acts of kindness and bravery can change the course of history.

Conclusion

Heroism is built on the foundation of sacrifice, resilience, perseverance, and vision. The heroes of WWII were a diverse group from varying backgrounds, yet they shared the common goal of liberating the world from the demonic tyranny of an unspeakable evil. Although the German war machine had advanced engineering and elite discipline, a few great people stood up and fought regardless of the odds. With unity and commitment to a virtuous goal, there is no telling how far you can go. The heroism of those who dedicated their lives to liberty and equality inspired many to join the fight, stand up, and defend justice.

The post-war reality was that new institutions were set up to ensure humanity did not descend into the chaotic path of destruction. A new awareness of the havoc humans are capable of awakened people to do whatever it takes to maintain peace. As political instability takes society to the brink of global conflict, it is now more critical than ever to remind people of the ideals of these heroes so humanity can step back from the brink.

Many of these heroes were flawed, but to stand up for an ideological goal more substantial than yourself, perfection is not required. Nothing would ever get done if everyone waited until they were perfect before doing anything. The bravery to courageously march into the unknown without a clue of the outcome, with nothing but grit and belief in your heart, can reshape the world for the better.

The contributions of the heroes named in this book and the anonymous heroes lost to the passage of time shaped a freer world with greater respect for human life. Globally, there is a long way to go before humanity reaches the pinnacle of a moral existence. But people will only get there with the guidance of those willing to stare down injustice and take action to stop it in its tracks, even at great personal loss. Civilization owes much to the war heroes on the frontlines and civilians who helped the most oppressed, knowing that it could cost them their lives and liberty.

These heroes are undoubtedly exceptional people, but the world can be a much better place by embodying even a fraction of their selfless commitment to a higher vision. As society collectively paves the way to a new world where each individual contributes to creating, look back and ask what the highest values are that can propel humankind into the stratosphere. A brilliant place to start looking for these values is in the murky darkness of WWII, where adversity and atrocity gave birth to some of the most remarkable people the world has ever had the pleasure of hosting.

Check out another book in the series

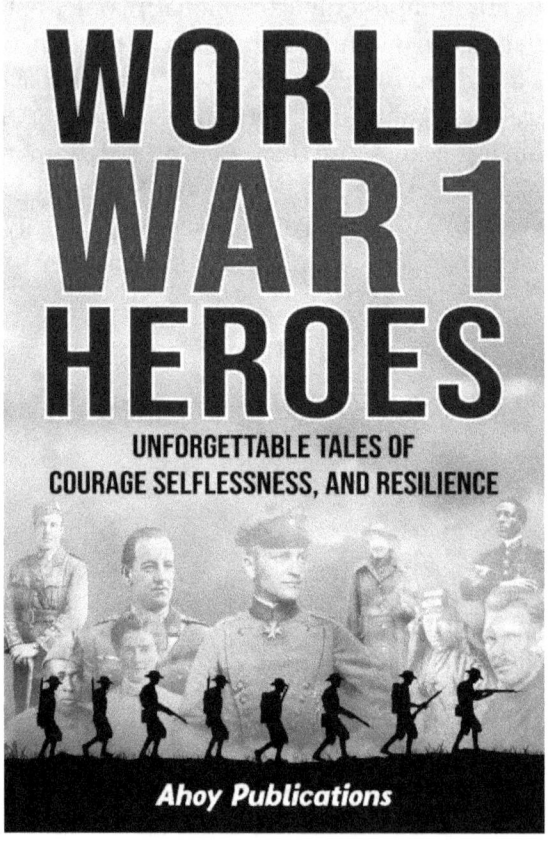

References

Alchetron. (2017, August 18). Vasily Zaytsev ~ Life Story & Biography with Photos | Videos. Alchetron. https://alchetron.com/Vasily-Zaytsev

Ambrose, S. E. (1992). Band Of Brothers: The Island. World War II History Info. https://worldwar2history.info/band-of-brothers/company.html

Arbuckle, A. (2017, November 28). The Navajo code talkers that helped the U.S. win WWII. Mashable. https://mashable.com/feature/navajo-code-talkers

Arlington National Cemetery. (2019). Audie Murphy. Arlington National Cemetery. https://www.arlingtoncemetery.mil/Explore/Notable-Graves/Medal-of-Honor-Recipients/World-War-II-MoH-recipients/Audie-Murphy

Audie Leon Murphy. (2017, February 22). Association of the United States Army. https://www.ausa.org/audie-leon-murphy

Audie Murphy's Military Decorations. (n.d.). Audie L. Murphy Memorial Website. https://www.audiemurphy.com/decorations.htm

Australian War Memorial. (2011). Nancy Grace Augusta "The White Mouse" Wake. Australian War Memorial. https://www.awm.gov.au/collection/P332

Bamford, T. (2020, January 26). Audie Murphy Single-handedly Stopped a German Attack. The National WWII Museum | New Orleans. https://www.nationalww2museum.org/war/articles/audie-murphy-single-handedly-stopped-german-attack

Bastogne Summary - Fort Campbell Historical Foundation. (2022, December 16). Fort Campbell Historical Foundation. https://fortcampbell.com/bastogne-summary/

Black History. (n.d.). Tuskegee Airmen. Black History. https://www.blackhistory.mit.edu/story/tuskegee-airmen

Black Past. (n.d.). The Tuskegee Airmen on BlackPast.org •. Black Past. https://www.blackpast.org/african-american-history/tuskegee-airmen-blackpast-org/#:~:text=The%20Tuskegee%20Airmen%20were%20the

Burkholder, A. (2018). Nancy Wake: The White Mouse - Heroine of World War II. Utah Historical Society. https://history.utah.gov/wp-content/uploads/2022/07/Nancy-Wake-The-White-Mouse.pdf

Burton, K. (n.d.). The Scientific and Technological Advances of World War II. The National WWII Museum. https://www.nationalww2museum.org/war/articles/scientific-and-technological-advances-world-war-ii

Collins, J. (2022, May 17). Greatest Marksmen: Vasily Zaitsev - Sonoran Desert Institute. Sonoran Desert Institute - School of Firearms Technology. https://www.sdi.edu/greatest-marksmen-vasily-zaitsev/

Cross, N. (2021, June 17). Research Guides: Navajo Code Talkers: A Guide to First-Person Narratives in the Veterans History Project: Introduction. Library of Congress. https://guides.loc.gov/navajo-code-talkers

Curran, C. (2016). Nancy Wake by Chloe Curran – Her Place Women's Museum. Her Place Museum. https://herplacemuseum.com/encounters/nancywake/

Curry, P. (2018, October 31). Vasily Zaytsev – The Enemy at the Gates. History Hit. https://www.historyhit.com/vasily-zaytsev-the-enemy-at-the-gates/

Days of Remembrance- The Irena Sendler's Story. (2023, April 4). DVIDS. https://www.dvidshub.net/video/878965/days-remembrance-irena-sendlers-story

FEATURE: Story of Japan's "Schindler" offers lessons for tackling contemporary xenophobia. (2017, January 26). UN News. https://news.un.org/en/story/2017/01/550292-feature-story-japans-schindler-offers-lessons-tackling-contemporary-xenophobia

Fitzgerald, C. (2023, August 30). The Post-War Lives of Easy Company's Famed Paratroopers. War History Online. https://www.warhistoryonline.com/world-war-ii/easy-company-members.html

FitzSimons, P. (2011, August 8). The White Mouse Who Roared. The Sydney Morning Herald. https://www.smh.com.au/world/the-white-mouse-who-roared-20110808-1ij2o.html

Global Security. (n.d.). Vasily Zaitsev. Global Security. https://www.globalsecurity.org/military/world/russia/zaitsev.htm

GOV.UK. (2018). History of Sir Winston Churchill. Www.gov.uk. https://www.gov.uk/government/history/past-prime-ministers/winston-churchill

Green, D. B. (2019, July 29). Who Is Chiune Sugihara? The Japanese Hero Who Saved 6,000 Jews From the Holocaust. Haaretz.

https://www.haaretz.com/world-news/2019-07-29/ty-article/.premium/chiune-sugihara-the-japanese-hero-who-saved-6-000-jews-from-the-holocaust/0000017f-f73b-d887-a7ff-ffff9e2b0000

Haley. (2013, May 21). Irena Sendler. The MY HERO Project. https://myhero.com/I_Sendler_dnhs_kt_US_2013_ul

Haskew, M. E. (2020). Operation Market Garden: The American Airborne's Audacious Role. Warfare History Network. https://warfarehistorynetwork.com/article/operation-market-garden-american-airborne-audacious-role/

Hayward, S. F. (2011, March 17). Chart of Achievements. International Churchill Society. https://winstonchurchill.org/resources/reference/chart-of-achievements/

Hemenway, M. (2023, September 13). Band Of Brothers Ending Explained: The Aftermath Of Easy Company After WWII. ScreenRant. https://screenrant.com/band-of-brothers-ending-explained/

Hernon, M. (2021, June 7). Spotlight: Chiune Sugihara - The Japanese Schindler. Tokyo Weekender. https://www.tokyoweekender.com/art_and_culture/japanese-culture/chiune-sugihara-japanese-schindler/

History, W. (2021, March 28). Vasilly Zaitsev - The Legendary Soviet Sniper From the Battle of Stalingrad. - Real History Online. Real History Online. https://www.realhistoryonline.com/operations-battles/vasilly-zaitsev-ww2-sniper/

History.com Editors. (2009, October 27). D-Day. History. https://www.history.com/topics/world-war-ii/d-day

History.com Editors. (2018, August 21). Raoul Wallenberg - Biography, Heroism & Disappearance. HISTORY. https://www.history.com/topics/holocaust/wallenberg-raoul

History.com. (2018, August 21). Battle of the Bulge. HISTORY. https://www.history.com/topics/world-war-ii/battle-of-the-bulge

How D-Day Was Fought From The Air. (2018). Imperial War Museums. https://www.iwm.org.uk/history/how-d-day-was-fought-from-the-air

Imperial War Museums. (2018). How Winston Churchill And The Conservative Party Lost The 1945 Election. Imperial War Museums. https://www.iwm.org.uk/history/how-winston-churchill-and-the-conservative-party-lost-the-1945-election

Imperial War Museums. (n.d.). The Story Of Operation "Market Garden" In Photos. Imperial War Museums. https://www.iwm.org.uk/history/the-story-of-operation-market-garden-in-photos

Jackl, K. (n.d.). Irena Sendler. Google Arts & Culture. https://artsandculture.google.com/story/irena-sendler-the-museum-of-the-history-of-polish-jews-jewish-museum-warsaw/zgWx_XNxPh8dLQ?hl=en

Johnson, L. (2022, September 28). 10 facts about SOE agent Nancy Wake. History Hit. https://www.historyhit.com/facts-about-soe-agent-nancy-wake/

Katie. (2021, February 3). Irena Sendler: The Angel of Warsaw. Girl Museum. https://www.girlmuseum.org/irena-sendler-the-angel-of-warsaw/

Koontz, C. (n.d.). Tuskegee Airmen. Air Force Historical Support Division. https://www.afhistory.af.mil/FAQs/Fact-Sheets/Article/458979/tuskegee-airmen/

Lukas, R. C. (2020, May 15). Irena Sendler: World War II's Polish Angel. Franciscan Media. https://www.franciscanmedia.org/st-anthony-messenger/irena-sendler-world-war-ii-s-polish-angel/

Macdonald, C. B. (n.d.). Operation MARKET-GARDEN. U.S. Army Center of Military History. https://history.army.mil/books/70-7_19.htm

Martin, P. (2020, July 19). Critical Mass: Unassuming Audie Murphy, a true American hero. Arkansas Online. https://www.arkansasonline.com/news/2020/jul/19/unassuming-audie-murphy-a-true-american-hero/

Mendes, C. (2019, February 9). The Mythical German Sniper From the "Enemy at the Gates" Who Challenged Vasily Zaitsev. War History Online. https://www.warhistoryonline.com/world-war-ii/the-truth-about-erwin-konig-sent-to-stalingrad-to-take-on-the-very-effective-soviet-snipers.html

Ministry of Foreign Affairs of Japan. (n.d.). MOFA: Story of a courageous diplomat of humanity, Mr. Chiune Sugihara. Ministry of Foreign Affairs of Japan. https://www.mofa.go.jp/region/middle_e/israel/sugihara.html

Mitchell, R. M. (1986). The 101st airborne division's defense of Bastogne.

National Archives and Records Administration. (2024). A People at War. Archives. https://www.archives.gov/exhibits/a_people_at_war/war_in_europe/101st_airborne_division.html

National Museum Of The United States Air Force. (2015, May). War of Secrets: Cryptology in WWII. National Museum of the US Air Force. https://www.nationalmuseum.af.mil/Visit/Museum-Exhibits/Fact-Sheets/Display/Article/196193/war-of-secrets-cryptology-in-wwii/

Neikirk, T. (2022, March 17). Vasily Zaytsev Allegedly Took Out One of Germany's Best Snipers. War History Online. https://www.warhistoryonline.com/war-articles/vasily-zaytsev.html

Oliver, A. E. (2017, December 7). Audie Murphy: Soldier, Once and forever. The MY HERO Project. https://myhero.com/audie-murphy-soldier-once-and-forever

Operation Market Garden. (n.d.). Liberation Route.
https://www.liberationroute.com/themed-routes/19/operation-market-garden

Paris, J. (n.d.). 1942: Navajo Code Talkers. Www.intelligence.gov.
https://www.intelligence.gov/people/barrier-breakers-in-history/453-navajo-code-talkers

Polonsky, A. (2008, May 14). Obituary: Irena Sendler. The Guardian.
https://www.theguardian.com/world/2008/may/14/secondworldwar.poland

Potts, J. (2019, April 9). World War Two: Street Snipers in the Battle of Stalingrad. History Is Now Magazine.
https://www.historyisnowmagazine.com/blog/2019/4/3/world-war-two-street-snipers-in-the-battle-of-stalingrad

Rankin, J. (2020, January 4). My Father, the Quiet Hero: How Japan's Schindler Saved 6,000 Jews. The Guardian.
https://www.theguardian.com/world/2020/jan/04/chiune-sugihara-my-father-japanese-schindler-saved-6000-jews-lithuania

Raoul Wallenberg Institute. (2019). About Raoul Wallenberg - Raoul Wallenberg Institute. Raoul Wallenberg Institute. https://rwi.lu.se/about/about-raoul-wallenberg/

Raoul Wallenberg. (2014, December 3). Sweden.
https://sweden.se/life/people/raoul-wallenberg-world-war-ii-hero

Shircliff, J. (2014). Women of the 1913 Armory Show: their contributions to the development of American modern art.
https://ir.library.louisville.edu/cgi/viewcontent.cgi?article=2321&context=etd

Silversmith, S. (2018, July 11). Navajo Code Talkers created an unbreakable code. It helped win World War II. Arizona Central.
https://www.azcentral.com/story/news/local/arizona/2018/07/11/navajo-code-talker-facts-unbreakable-code/460262002/

Smith, D. A. (2015, June 3). Historian: Audie Murphy, Movie Star and WWII's Most Decorated Hero, Suffered from PTSD. Baylor University.
https://news.web.baylor.edu/news/story/2015/historian-audie-murphy-movie-star-and-wwiis-most-decorated-hero-suffered-ptsd

Tapalaga, A. (2022, December 20). Vasily Zaitsev: The Fear of The German Army. History of Yesterday. https://historyofyesterday.com/vasily-zaitsev-the-fear-of-the-german-army/

The 101st Airborne Division. (n.d.). Holocaust Encyclopedia.
https://encyclopedia.ushmm.org/content/en/article/the-101st-airborne-division

The National WWII Museum. (n.d.). The African American Pilots of WWII.
https://www.nationalww2museum.org/sites/default/files/2017-07/tuskegee-airmen.pdf

The Nobel Prize in Literature 1953. (2019). Nobel Prize. https://www.nobelprize.org/prizes/literature/1953/churchill/biographical/

The Role the 82d & 101st Airborne Divisions Played During the Holocaust | ASOMF. (2021, March 6). Www.asomf.org. https://www.asomf.org/the-role-the-82d-101st-airborne-divisions-played-during-the-holocaust/

The Royal Mint. (n.d.). 10 facts about Winston Churchill | The Royal Mint. Royal Mint. https://www.royalmint.com/stories/collect/10-facts-about-winston-churchill/

This Soviet Sniper Was A Nazi-Killing Machine with 242 Confirmed Kills in 4 Months. (n.d.). Atchuup. https://www.atchuup.com/vasily-zaytsev-nazi-killing-machine/

United States Holocaust Memorial Museum. (2019). Chiune (Sempo) Sugihara. United States Holocaust Memorial Museum. https://encyclopedia.ushmm.org/content/en/article/chiune-sempo-sugihara

University, T. (2019). Tuskegee Airmen Facts. Tuskegee University. https://www.tuskegee.edu/support-tu/tuskegee-airmen/tuskegee-airmen-facts

Vasily Zaitsev. (n.d.). Russiapedia. https://russiapedia.rt.com/prominent-russians/military/vasily-zaitsev/

Wallenberg Legacy. (n.d.). The Story of Raoul Wallenberg. Wallenberg Legacy. https://wallenberg.umich.edu/raoul-wallenberg/the-story-of-raoul-wallenberg/

Wenjie, W., & Wang, K. (n.d.). Nancy Wake (1912-2011). https://www.mindef.gov.sg/oms/safti/pointer/documents/pdf/Vol42No2_8%20Nancy%20Wake.pdf

Willsher, K. (2011, August 8). Farewell to Nancy Wake, the Mouse Who Ran Rings Around the Nazis. The Guardian. https://theguardian.com/world/2011/aug/08/nancy-wake-white-mouse-gestapo

www.ingramcontent.com/pod-product-compliance
Lightning Source LLC
Chambersburg PA
CBHW070729130626
46553CB00005B/2205